THE INCOMPLETE CHURCH

BRIDGING THE GAP BETWEEN GOD'S CHILDREN

Sid Roth

DESTINY IMAGE® PUBLISHERS, INC.
P.O. Box 310, Shippensburg, PA 17257-0310

"Speaking to the Purposes of God for this Generation and for the Generations to Come."

This book and all other Destiny Image, Revival Press, Mercy Place, Fresh Bread, Destiny Image Fiction, and Treasure House books are available at Christian bookstores and distributors worldwide.

For a U.S. bookstore nearest you, call 1-800-722-6774. For more information on foreign distributors, call 717-532-3040. Or reach us on the Internet: www.destinyimage.com

ISBN 10: 0-7684-2437-2

ISBN 13: 978-0-7684-2437-9

For Worldwide Distribution, Printed in the U.S.A.

5 6 7 8 9 10 11 / 09 08

ENDORSEMENTS

"Sid's insights are powerful and illuminating. They reveal that we must bridge the gap and tear down the dividing walls between Christians and the Jewish people to release the End-Time power of God to the entire world."

—Larry Huch,
Pastor, DFW New Beginnings, Irving, Texas

The Incomplete Church gives us a true vision of eternity—an eternity where Jew and Gentile become one."

—Gordon Robertson,
Co-Host and Executive Producer, The 700 Club

DEDICATIONS

To my daughter, Leigh, and son-in-law, Greg Williamson. Leigh is Jewish, and Greg is a Gentile. Both know and love the Messiah of Israel. (My first grand-daughter is named Olivia because she is the fruit of the Jew and Gentile grafted into the Olive Tree.)

ACKNOWLEDGEMENT

I also wish to thank Robert DuVall who has spent many hours editing the manuscript. He has been a trusted friend and a real "Timothy" to me over the years.

CONTENTS

FOREWORD

I met Sid Roth at a service in Jacksonville, Florida, where my wife, Kathy, and I were ministering. Sid was so hungry for a touch from God that he shook under the power of the Holy Spirit. As I've watched Sid over the years, I've seen his passion for the deeper things of the Lord increase the mantle to bring a fresh move of God into the Jewish community. Many of Sid's insights in this book bridge the great chasm between the Church and the Jewish people. As the bridge is built, bringing Jewish and non-Jewish people together, we are prepared to take the next step in fulfilling God's purposes in this last hour.

Although the Jewish people are important to what God is doing in the earth, they have suffered greatly from anti-Semitism promulgated by some of the early Church leaders. This book reveals the roots of anti-Semitism in the Church and prophetically proclaims an outline for the next great move of God.

I agree wholeheartedly with Sid that the Church is incomplete without Jewish believers coming together with non-Jewish believers, as they did in the Book of Acts. Most Christians don't realize that the first apostles and leaders were Jews who evangelized the non-Jewish world. Now is the time for Gentiles to return the favor by letting the glory of God flow through us back to the Jewish people.

This book is part of something I have longed for and dreamed of for many years—to see Jewish apostles and prophets again walking the earth. As these Jewish leaders are raised up and released, we will see the end-time Church become "One New Man," manifesting the glory of God. Ephesians 4:4-6 states:

> *We are all one body, we have the same Spirit, and we have all been called to the same glorious future. There is only one Lord, one faith, one baptism, and there is only one God and Father, who is over us all and in us all and living through us all* (NLT).

Messiah Jesus has broken down the middle wall of division between Jew and Gentile. (See Ephesians 2:14.) When the two come together creating One New Man, the glory will increase with healings, miracles, and the greatest harvest of souls in history.

—Steve Gray
World Revival Church, Kansas City, Missouri
(Former pastor of the Smithton Outpouring)

1

THE JEWISH COVENANT

IS CHRISTIANITY JEWISH? We know Jesus was born a Jew. He lived a Jewish life and died as a Jew. The Cross held this inscription: "THIS IS JESUS THE KING OF THE JEWS" (Matt. 27:37). Jesus said the New Covenant was *only* for the Jewish people (see Matt. 15:24). Jeremiah prophesied the same thing. *"Behold, the days are coming, says the Lord, when I will make a **new covenant** with the house of **Israel** and the house of **Judah**"* (Jer. 31:31).

This new covenant was not with the Gentiles. It was only with the Jewish people. The only way a Gentile could be saved was to be converted to Judaism. But God loved the whole world and gave us many prophecies about the gathering of the Gentiles. *"Then I will say to those who were not My people, 'You are My people!' And they shall say, 'You are my God!'"* (Hos. 2:23).

Paul says of the Gentiles in Ephesians 2:12, *"At that time you were without Christ, being aliens from the **commonwealth of Israel** and **strangers from the*** *covenants....*" *Commonwealth of Israel* could be translated "freedom of Israel." I love the freedom God grants Jew and Gentile in the Messiah. It is not legalism, as you will see, but *freedom!* When you are no longer *strangers from the covenants* of Israel, you will know the truth, and the truth will result in freedom and friendship with God.

Ruth, a Gentile, was a prophetic picture of this freedom for the Gentiles. She said to her Jewish mother-in-law, Naomi, "...*Your people shall be my people, and your God, my God*" (Ruth 1:16). The meaning of *Ruth* is "friend." When she entered the Jewish covenant, she became a friend of God and a friend of the Jewish people. She married the Jew, Boaz, and their union produced a great-grandson named David—who would become King David.

Paul explains the grafting of the Gentiles into the Jewish covenant using the analogy of the olive tree. The olive tree is a type of Israel. We know this because Paul, speaking of the Jewish people in Romans 11:24, called it *"their own olive tree."* The "natural branches" are the Jewish people, and the "wild branches" are the Gentiles. Paul says that the Gentiles are grafted into a Jewish olive tree.

Does this mean that a Gentile Christian physically becomes a Jew or a part of Israel (see Chapter 4)? No! Although both branches share equally in the covenants, we have unique callings. Just as a husband

and wife are one and equal in the marriage covenant, they have different callings. The Bible gives instructions to husbands that are different from the instructions for wives. Let's look at some of the promises to the Jewish people that are part of their calling:

God promises to give the land of Israel forever to the Jewish people through Abraham, Isaac, and Jacob.

[To Abraham] *Also I give to you and your descendants after you the land in which you are a stranger, all the land of Canaan, as an everlasting possession...* (Genesis 17:8).

[To Isaac] *Dwell in this land, and I will be with you and bless you; for to you and your descendants I give all these lands, and I will perform the oath which I swore to Abraham your father* (Genesis 26:3).

[To Jacob] *And* [God will] *give you the blessing of Abraham, to you and your descendants with you, that you may inherit the land in which you are a stranger, which God gave to Abraham* (Genesis 28:4).

God also promises to judge the nations according to their treatment of Israel and the Jewish people.

I will also gather all nations...and I will enter into judgment with them there on account of My people, My heritage Israel...(Joel 3:2).

Similarly, God promises to bless those who bless the Jewish people and curse those who curse them.

> *I will bless those who bless you, and I will curse him who curses you* (Genesis 12:3).

He also promises to re-gather the Jewish people to the land of Israel.

> *'The Lord lives who brought up the children of Israel from the land of the north and from all the lands where He had driven them.' For I will bring them back into their land which I gave to their fathers* (Jeremiah 16:15).

While the Bible makes many promises to the Jewish people, the *greater end-time call belongs to Gentile believers.* They are called to lead the Jewish people to Jesus. *"To provoke them* [the Jew] *to jealousy, salvation has come to the Gentiles"* (Rom. 11:11b). When the Jew and Gentile converge together as One New Man, it will spark an end-time revival such as the world has never seen.

Merriam-Webster defines *convergence* as "the act of converging and especially moving toward union... coordinated movement of the two eyes so that the image of a *single point* is formed on corresponding retinal areas" (emphasis added).[1] The world cannot clearly see Jesus until Jew and Gentile converge into the One New Man. Deuteronomy 32:30 tells us what will happen when the convergence fully manifests: *"How could one chase a thousand, and two* [Jew and Gentile] *put ten thousand to flight...?"*

A foretaste of what will happen when the ancient Jewish anointing merges with the Christian anointing is found in the description of the millennial river in Ezekiel 47:9: *"And wherever the double* [Jew and Christian] *river shall go,* **every** *living creature which swarms shall live. And there shall be a very great number of fish* [revival]..." (AMP). This convergence will cause a healing anointing to rise from ankle depth to total saturation (see Ezek. 47:3-5). This convergence will be exponential. *It will change the face of the Church forever!*

God wants to *"gather together in* **one** *all things in* [the Messiah]" (Eph. 1:10). He tells us how He will do this:

> *For He Himself is our peace, who has made both [Jew and Gentile]* **one,** *and has broken down the middle wall of separation...to create in Himself* **one new man**.... *In whom you also are being built together for a* **dwelling place** *of God in the Spirit (Ephesians 2:14-15,22).*

What is at stake in this convergence of Jew and Gentile? Nothing short of the salvation of the world.

Jesus summarized God's winning strategy when He expressed His desire that *"they all may be one...**that the world may believe**..."* (John 17:21). I believe *"they"* refers to Jew and Gentile—the only two people groups at that time.

Further, the same glory that is on Jesus will be on the One New Man. Jesus said, *"The glory which You gave Me I have given them, that they* [Jew and Gentile] *may be one just as We are one"* (John 17:22). God is up to something new, something fresh. It is the convergence of Jew and Gentile in Jesus to form the One New Man.

2

"WE ARE NOT LOST"

IT IS A MIRACLE that Jewish people still exist today. After thousands of years of persecution, there should be none left. But God said that as long as there is a sun and moon and stars, at least one physical Jew will remain on the face of the earth (see Jer. 31:35-36).

We know that during His millennial reign, Jesus and His disciples will rule over the twelve tribes of Israel (see Matt. 19:28). The ancient rabbis believed that three things had to take place before the Messiah would appear. First, Israel had to be restored as a Jewish nation, which occurred in 1948. Second, the temple had to be rebuilt in Jerusalem. This could happen very quickly. And third, the ten lost tribes had to be restored to Israel (see Jer. 31:7-11). This seemed impossible—until now.

Filmmaker Simcha Jacobovici, a traditional Jew, read about the locations where the lost tribes were scattered in Isaiah 11:11. He set up an exploratory expedition to find and document the existence of these tribes. Not only did he find them exactly where God had scattered them, but he also discovered that they had not assimilated into their surrounding environments.

For example, he found descendants from the tribe of Manasseh living in northeast India. They observe the Sabbath, the festivals, and the biblical Jewish laws. In 2000, the Israeli Ministry of the Interior granted citizenship to the first one hundred members of that tribe.

All ten "lost" tribes have been located. They say, "We are not lost!" Many of the tribes practice an aberrant form of Judaism, but all have relics and customs proving their heritage. I agree with them and the Word of God—they are not lost.

Everlasting Covenant of Love

God loves Israel. He made an everlasting covenant of love that no person or thing can break. In Romans 11:28-29, Paul states:

Concerning the gospel [the Jewish people] *are enemies for your sake* [so that the Gentiles can be saved], *but concerning the election they are beloved for the sake of the fathers. For the gifts and the calling of God are* **irrevocable.**

God's covenant love for the Jewish people is further evident in Hosea. God said:

> *When Israel was a child, I loved him....They sacrificed to the Baals, and burned incense to carved images. I taught Ephraim* [Israel] *to walk, taking them by their arms.... I drew them with gentle cords, with bands of love.... I stooped and fed them.... How can I give you up, Ephraim?...My heart churns within Me* (Hos. 11:1-4,8).

God cries out to Israel, saying, *"Return, O backsliding children...for I am married to you...and I will bring you to Zion* [Israel]*"* (Jer. 3:14).

If God refuses to violate His covenant love for His ancient Jewish people, even in the face of their disobedience, imagine the love that He has for His New Covenant people. God says to the older brother (symbolic of the Gentile believer) in the parable of the prodigal son, *"All that I have is yours"* (Luke 15:31).

No Jews Allowed

Throughout history, people like Haman in the Book of Esther, Queen Isabella of Spain, and Adolf Hitler have cursed the Jews. Entire nations have come against the Jewish people. This is true even here in America, "the land of the free." I remember, as a young child, seeing a sign at the beach that read, "No Dogs or Blacks or Jews Allowed!" (Except, it used a different word for *Blacks*.)

What is the result of these curses against Jews? Jewish people as a whole are spiritually blind to the gospel message. The devil has backed Jews into a corner. We have bitterness, pain, and hatred in our hearts. Our response is understandable. We blamed God for the Holocaust. We blamed Christians for our persecution. We are painfully aware of the tragic history of anti-Semitism among many Church fathers. Even for Jews who love God, these wounds are buried deep in our psyches.

How then can Christian believers reach the Jewish people with the gospel? One of the best methods is through a miracle of physical healing. Paul emphasizes this method in First Corinthians 1:22, saying, *"The Jews request a sign...."* I have conducted lectures on the supernatural in Berlin, Germany, Haifa, Israel, and many places in the former Soviet Union. Unsaved Jews filled these theaters, and when they witnessed the supernatural signs, large numbers of them came to know Jesus as Messiah.

But there is an even greater way. Malachi 4:5-6 says that Elijah will prepare the way for the Messiah. The Spirit that was on Elijah will come upon the Church, and allow it to walk in the pure love of God. Many spiritual fathers will be raised up. The Gentile Christian has a heritage of 2,000 years of walking with Jesus. We Jewish people are incomplete without you. Your calling is to reveal the love of the heavenly Father *to the Jew first* and then to the entire world (see Chapter 10). Only the compassion of Father God will melt the deep wounding in Jewish hearts.

Standing With the Jewish People

The Jews are the most love-starved people on the face of the earth; they have been regularly abused, misunderstood, persecuted, discriminated against, and murdered. We have a covenant with God, but most Jews do not know Him. As a result, many of my people are on the forefront of unbiblical positions, supporting pro-abortion, pro-homosexual rights, and pro-New Age movements while standing against school prayer.

But even in our state of being separated from God because of sin, the blessings from God are still on the Jew. *"For the gifts and the calling of God are irrevocable"* (Rom. 11:29).

Author Robert Heidler writes: "Whether the field is music, art, entertainment, business or science; the Jews have influenced our lives and culture as no other ethnic group of comparable size. Names like…Albert Einstein, Carl Sagan, Isaac Asimov, Arthur Miller,

Alan Greenspan, Rogers and Hammerstein, and Irving Berlin are so much a part of our American vocabulary, most of us don't even stop to think that these American icons are all Jewish."[1] In his book, *The Jewish Phenomenon*, Steven Silberger notes that 20% of professors at leading American universities are Jewish along with 25% of American Nobel Prize winners.[2] Paul says that "...if [the Jewish people's] *fall is riches for the world...how much more their fullness!*" (Rom. 11:12).

The devil's strategy is to use the anti-God stances of some Jews to cause nominal Christians to join unbelievers in hating *all* Jews. The world and *nominal* Christians will also hate genuine Christian believers. First they will hate them for standing with the Jew. Then they will hate them for standing with the Jewish Messiah. First the natural, then the spiritual. Christians need to heed the warning that Mordecai gave Esther:

> *Do not think in your heart that you will escape in the king's palace any more than all the other Jews. For if you remain completely silent at this time, relief and deliverance will arise for the Jews from another place, but you and your father's house will perish...* (Esther 4:13-14).

Standing with the Jew is not a popular decision, but "if God is for you, who can be against you?" (see Rom.

8:31). God has faith in you. He is passionately and patiently waiting for this last generation to demonstrate His words in Isaiah 49:22-23:

> *Thus says the Lord God: "Behold, I will lift My hand in an oath to the nations* [Gentiles], *and set up My standard for the peoples; they shall bring your sons* [Jewish people] *in their arms, and your daughters shall be carried on their shoulders; kings shall be your foster fathers, and their queens your nursing mothers; they shall bow down to you with their faces to the earth, and lick up the dust of your feet. Then you will know that I am the Lord...."*

Jewish people will know that Jesus is the Messiah when all Christian believers (kings and queens in God's Kingdom) start acting like disciples (by surrendering to the Lordship of Jesus) and stop conforming to the world. The world will hate you, but the multitudes that will be in heaven because you obeyed God's commands will welcome you home.

3

THE RABBINIC CONSPIRACY

A FRIEND OF MINE, the pastor of a large Charismatic church, had a supernatural experience while visiting the Great Synagogue in Jerusalem. As he was praying, Jesus came to him and said, "I would be more at home in this building than in your church."

Although many Gentile believers long for a deeper walk with God, many do not recognize that they are missing their biblical, Jewish heritage. Is the solution to add Rabbinic Judaism to our present dogma? No. Simply put, Rabbinic Judaism has drifted far from the Judaism of the Bible. Tradition in the Church may have isolated Christians from their Jewish roots and from experiencing the full intimacy and power of God (see Chapter 12), but the tradition of the rabbis has separated Jewish people from their Messiah.

While the devil was deceiving the Church leaders with anti-Semitic thoughts, he was also corrupting the authority of the Scriptures in Judaism. Both groups dug in and believed the big lie—you cannot be Jewish and believe in Jesus. The formula was simple. Give the rabbis authority *above* the Scriptures, remove Jesus from Judaism, and separate the Christian from the Jew. This will stop the unlimited outpouring of God's glory, and the full revival will be aborted.

Judaism Repackaged

Let us examine how Rabbinic Judaism has tried to exclude Jesus. In the Great Revolt by Jewish zealots against Roman rule (A.D. 66–70), a million Jews were killed and the temple in Jerusalem was destroyed. Afterward, Yohanan ben Zakkai set about to reconstruct Judaism in Yavne, along the coast of Israel. Why was this necessary? Because the temple no longer existed and they had rejected God's Messiah—the sacrifice that was made once for all. The Torah (first five books of the Old Covenant) clearly says that without the shedding of blood, there is no remission of sin (see Lev. 17:11). Rather than accept the truth that animal sacrifices were a shadow of the ultimate Passover Lamb—the Messiah—who would take away all sin, ben Zakkai and his followers invented a new, bloodless religion—Rabbinic Judaism. The following story illustrates the dramatic shift that took place within Judaism:

As Rabban Yohanan ben Zakkai was coming forth

from Jerusalem, Rabbi Joshua followed after him and beheld the Temple in ruins. "Woe unto us!" Rabbi Joshua cried, "that this, the place where the iniquities of Israel were atoned for, is laid waste!" "My son," Rabban Yohanan said to him, "be not grieved; we have another atonement as effective as this. And what is it? It is acts of loving-kindness, as it is said, *'For I desire mercy and not sacrifice'* [Hosea 6:6]" (Avot de Rabbi Nathan 4:18).[1]

At the end of his life, ben Zakkai finally realized that his creation gave him no assurance of life after death. On his deathbed, he said, "I have before me two roads, one to Paradise and one to Gehenna [hell], and I know not whether [God] will sentence me to Gehenna or admit me to Paradise" (Tractate Berachot 28b). A famous Rabbi once said, "If the blind leads the blind, both will fall into a ditch" (see Matt. 15:14).

Rabbi Akiba ben Joseph studied the teachings of Yohanan ben Zakkai in Yavne and continued to build on his foundation. He created the structure of the Talmud, which is a declaration of rabbinic authority. Although the Talmud contains a good deal of wisdom and godly teaching, one of the major goals of its authors was to keep the Jews from believing in Messiah Jesus. It distorts many of the Messianic interpretations of the Jewish Scriptures. There is clear evidence that *before* Jesus came to earth, the Jewish people were expecting a Messiah and interpreted the Messianic prophecies without bias.

Today, the rabbis claim that the Talmud, or Oral Law, came from God at the same time that the Written Law was given to Moses on Mount Sinai. This is not true. Even in the first century, Jewish leaders did not claim that the rabbinic law came from Sinai. Instead they spoke of "oral traditions." The Jewish Bible, the Dead Sea Scrolls, and the Jewish historian Josephus (A.D. 93) do not even mention an oral law.

The method of interpreting Scripture employed by Akiba and his followers rejected the rules of grammar and plain logic. Author Dan Gruber writes, "Sometimes the Rabbis were unable to read their teachings into the Scriptures by any means. So they simply annulled the decrees of Torah [first five books of the Old Covenant]."[2] They proclaimed rabbinic authority took precedence over the Scriptures.[3] The Talmud states, "My son, take heed of the words of the Scribes more than the words of the Torah" (Tractate Erubin 21b).[4] Akiba's objective was to bring the Jewish people under the rule of the rabbis.

The Talmud even says that if a voice from Heaven contradicts the majority of the rabbis, the rabbis are correct.[5] In other words, nobody is allowed to contradict the authority of the rabbis, not even God! Is it any wonder, then, considering the persecution from the Church, the lack of miracles and supernatural power in Christianity, and the rabbinic conspiracy, that the Jewish people know nothing about Jesus?

A sect of Judaism created this new rabbinic form but it is important to understand that at the time of Jesus' first coming *three* main sects existed within Judaism: Pharisees, Sadducees, and Essenes. These three disagreed on the core theological issues of Judaism.

Today we are most familiar with the view of the Pharisees. They believed that God had no triune nature and that the Word of God consisted of both the Old Covenant Scriptures (Tenach) and the oral traditions. They were looking for a Messiah who would initiate true peace and rule the world. The Pharisees are the fathers of modern-day Rabbinic Judaism.

The Sadducees only accepted the first five books of the Old Testament (Torah) as legal and binding. They rejected the resurrection of the dead and the existence of angels. They focused more on political matters than religious.

The Essenes were the largest Jewish sect during Jesus' earthly ministry. Most of the first Jewish followers of Jesus came from this sect. Why? The Dead Sea Scrolls tell us that the Essenes believed in the triune nature of God. They accepted the entire Tenach (Old

Covenant) as true, but rejected the Oral Law. The Essenes expected the appearance of an atoning Messiah. Messianic Jewish author Dr. Raymond Robert Fischer notes, "It was only the Essenes who had a clear understanding of Mashiyach's [Messiah's] absolute Divinity, precise sacrificial purpose, Davidic lineage and eschatological timing."[6] By understanding the Essenes, we see that Jesus the Messiah was the fulfillment of their expectations, not the founder of a new Gentile religion.

Who Is the Messiah?

In modern times, the rabbis have missed two of the most significant events that have happened to the Jewish people in the last 2,000 years. Messianic Jewish author Ron Cantor notes that many rabbis initially opposed the creation of Israel as a modern Jewish nation. "Many of the rabbis of Jerusalem were actually siding with the Arabs to keep this from happening. They believed only the Messiah could set up a Jewish state."[7] They also vehemently opposed Eliezer Ben Yehuda's plans in the late 1800s to restore Hebrew as the national language of the Jewish people. Cantor notes, "If it was so clear to the rabbis that both the Jewish state and the Hebrew language were the dreams of false prophets and yet they were wrong, it is possible that they also missed it on the single most important issue in Judaism—the Messiah!"[8]

Does Isaiah 53 Speak of Jesus?

Although Isaiah 53 is in the accepted Jewish Scriptures (Tenach), it is not part of the regular synagogue readings. Isaiah recorded this prophecy seven centuries before Jesus was born. Because it is not read in the synagogues, the Jewish people miss the most graphic description of Jesus in the Jewish Scriptures:

Who has believed our message and to whom has the arm of the Lord been revealed?...He had no beauty or majesty to attract us to Him, nothing in His appearance that we should desire Him. He was despised and rejected by men, a man of sorrows, and familiar with suffering. Like one from whom men hide their faces He was despised, and we esteemed Him not. Surely He took up our infirmities and carried our sorrows, yet we considered Him stricken by God, smitten by Him, and afflicted. But He was pierced for our transgressions, He was crushed for our iniquities; the punishment that brought us peace was upon Him, and by His wounds we are healed. We all, like sheep, have gone astray, each of us has turned to his own way; and the Lord has laid on Him the iniquity of us all (Isa. 53:1-6 NIV).

When I share this passage with rabbis, some say that they are not holy enough and must read what the rabbis in the past had to say about it. But they don't go back far enough. They only consult the rabbis after

Jesus—the ones who distorted the Messianic Scriptures. The rabbis before Jesus were not prejudiced and saw the Messianic significance of this passage.[9] Others try to make it sound as if the prophet is speaking of Israel rather than Jesus. Yet, Isaiah 53:8-9 says that the One who would die for the sins of the world would have no sin of His own. This could not be Israel. There are numerous places in Scripture where the prophets point out Israel's sins. No nation is sinless before God. When my own Orthodox Jewish father read Isaiah 53, he knew immediately that the prophet was describing Jesus—despite being taught all his life that Jesus was *not* the Jewish Messiah.

Think for Yourself

God made sure we could recognize the Messiah by giving us over 300 identifying marks, which were described by the prophets of Israel. In addition to the passage from Isaiah 53 quoted above, below are a few other prophecies about the Messiah from the Jewish Scriptures. Please take a moment to read through them and have your own God encounter.

Jeremiah predicted a new covenant that would wipe away sins and allow us to know (have intimacy with) God. *"The time is coming,"* declares the Lord, *"when I will make a new covenant with the house of Israel...and will remember their sins no more"* (Jer. 31:31,34 NIV).

The Jewish Scriptures also tell us that the Messiah would be born in Bethlehem.

> *But you, Bethlehem Ephrathah, though you are small among the clans of Judah, out of you will come for me one who will be ruler over Israel, whose origins are from of old, from ancient times* (Micah 5:2 NIV).

His ancestry would be from the family of David. *"'The days are coming,' declares the Lord, 'when I will raise up to David a righteous Branch....This is the name by which He will be called: The Lord Our Righteousness'"* (Jer. 23:5–6 NIV).

The Gentiles would also follow Him. *"In that day the Root of Jesse will stand as a banner for the peoples; the nations will rally to Him, and His place of rest will be glorious"* (Isa. 11:10 NIV).

He would die *before* the second temple was destroyed. *"...The Anointed One will be cut off and will have nothing. The people of the ruler who will come will destroy the city* [Jerusalem] *and the sanctuary..."* (Dan. 9:26 NIV).

He would also be raised from the dead. *"Because You will not abandon me to the grave, nor will You let your Holy One see decay"* (Ps. 16:10 NIV).

Since the temple was destroyed in A.D. 70, the Messiah had to come, die, and be resurrected before that time! What other person do you know who descended from King David, was born in Bethlehem, was followed by the Gentiles, was sacrificed for our sins before the destruction of the second temple, and was raised from the dead?

Since God has provided the blood of atonement through Messiah Jesus, we must repent (admit we have sinned and turn from unrighteousness) and ask for forgiveness in the name of Jesus. Each individual's prayer should be spoken out loud:

Messiah Jesus, I admit that I have sinned. I believe that You have provided the blood of atonement for me. With your help, I turn from my sins. I receive You now as my Messiah and Lord. Thank You for giving me shalom with God.

4

WHO IS ISRAEL?

MY FRIEND the late Dr. Derek Prince wrote, "Almost limitless misunderstanding, ignorance and distortion have pervaded the church for many centuries concerning the identity of Israel. This seems extraordinary to me because the statements in the Bible regarding Israel are so clear. Nevertheless, the minds of multitudes of Christians seem to be clouded in regard to the application of the name Israel."[1] Dr. Prince also said that a Christian who has no particular love for the Jew and Israel is "deficient" and "incomplete."[2]

So, who is Israel? Did the Jews forfeit their birthright to the Christians, just as Esau did to Jacob? Has the Christian Church replaced the Jews in God's sight? Hardly. This erroneous theology, known as Replacement Theology, is blinding many to the truth.

What Is Replacement Theology?

The core belief of Replacement Theology is that the Church has replaced Israel and the Jewish people in God's divine plan. This theology says that all the promises to Jews and Israel now belong exclusively to the Church. In other words, the Church gets all the blessings that really belong to the Jews.

In 1948, many of those who believed in Replacement Theology had a change of heart when the State of Israel was reestablished. They realized that God's promises were literal as well as spiritual. He never went back on His promises to the physical nation of Israel. Paul puts it this way: *"For the gifts and the calling of God are irrevocable"* (Rom. 11:29). The prophet Jeremiah writes, *"If heaven above can be measured, and the foundations of the earth searched out beneath, I will also cast off all the seed of Israel for all they have done, says the Lord"* (Jer. 31:37). If you can trust God with His promises to the Jewish people, you can trust Him with His promises to the Church!

Why Can't the Church Be the "New Israel"?

A fair reading of Romans 9–11 answers this question. For instance, Romans 11:28 talks about Israel. Some say it now means the Church and that the Church has replaced Israel. Let's insert the word *Church* instead of *Israel* and see how it reads:

"Concerning the gospel they [the Church] *are the enemies for your sake, but concerning the election they [the Church] are beloved for the sake of the fathers"* (Rom. 11:28). The Church is not God's enemy! The Church is not beloved for the promises to the fathers—Abraham, Isaac, and Jacob. The Jewish people are beloved for the sake of the promises to the Jewish fathers. Obviously, the Church has not replaced Israel.

Let's turn to a modern-day version found in *The Message,* for a clearer understanding of Romans 11:28-29:

> *From your point of view as you hear and embrace the good news of the Message, it looks like the Jews are God's enemies. But looked at from the long-range perspective of God's overall purpose, they remain God's oldest friends. God's gifts and God's call are under full warranty—never canceled, never rescinded.*

God's purpose was to reach His beloved—the Jews—first, and then the Gentiles. The Jewish people are forever beloved for the sake of God's promises to the Jewish forefathers.

Could *Jew* or *Israel* in Scripture sometimes refer to the Church? The terms *Jew* or *Jews* are found over 190 times in the New Testament. They are always used to describe the Jewish people. They never refer to a Gentile Christian. The 77 references to *Israel* always refer to the land of Israel or to the Jewish people.

But what about Galatians 3:28, "*...there is neither Jew nor Greek*"? Doesn't that mean there is no longer a special calling on the Jewish people? You must keep reading. The verse goes on to say "there is neither male nor female." Paul is saying that in Yeshua we are all the new creation, the Body of Messiah. But as long as this earth exists in the natural realm, there will be males and females, Jews and Gentiles. Although we become a new creation in Messiah, we still keep our own gender and ethnic identity. This is why James could address his letter to the twelve tribes (of Israel). He still saw Jewish believers as Israelites. In Romans 9:4, Paul even calls Jews who rejected the Messiah "Israelites." Paul refers to himself as a Jew after becoming a believer (see Acts 21:39). Although we are all equal, the Bible has different callings for males and females as well as Jews and Gentiles.

While the evidence against Replacement Theology is so clear-cut and overwhelming, there are more subtle, hybrid versions of the teaching that can be more difficult to spot.

What Is Two-Covenant Theology?

One is called Two-Covenant Theology. Many people who love the Jew cannot accept that those Jewish people who do not believe in Jesus will be eternally separated from God. They believe a Jew has a covenant with God that eliminates the necessity of believing in Jesus. This is not true. The Mosaic Covenant requires an animal sacrifice *in the temple* for forgiveness of sin. (See Leviticus 1:5; 17:11.) Since there is no temple, there can be no bloodshed for the atonement of sins. Hebrews 9:22 says, "…*Without shedding of blood there is **no remission*** [for sin]." Jesus died—once and for all—and rose again. He has paid the ultimate price by shedding His own blood. Therefore, He is the only way to salvation (see John 14:6).

Since there are no animal sacrifices, won't God accept repentance alone by a good, traditional Jew? No. Acts 4:12 says about belief in Jesus that "*there is no other name under heaven given among men by which we must be saved.*"

In Romans 11:26, Paul says that "*all Israel will be saved.*" So why witness to the Jewish people? Many Jewish people will die without knowing God *before* their national day of visitation. Only those who are *alive* in Israel at that time will be rescued.

What Is Two-House Theology?

An even subtler version of Replacement Theology is called Two-House Theology. This is based on the belief that the ten *northern* tribes of Israel are lost among the nations. Proponents believe that any Gentile Christian who follows the Torah (first five books of the Old Covenant) is part of these lost tribes.[3] They even call themselves "Israel" or "Ephraim." Furthermore, they say that the people who identify themselves as Jews today are really from the tribe of Judah (one of the *southern* tribes).

However, the fact that a Gentile Christian has a heart to follow the Torah does not make him a physical Jew. Many Christians have some Jewish blood in their ancestry. This does not necessarily make them Jewish either. I have an ancestor from Ireland five generations back. This does not make me Irish. Furthermore, the "lost tribes" are not lost. (See Chapter 2.) Researchers have identified living representatives of all the tribes of Israel.

Two-House Theology is also based on an allegorical, rather than literal, interpretation of Scripture. But we have no right to spiritualize God's Word if our interpretation contradicts the literal meaning.

Let's start with simple definitions. The word *Hebrew* was first used to identify Abram's (Abraham's) family (see Gen. 14:13). It was Abraham's grandson,

Jacob, who was first called *Israel* after he wrestled with God (see Gen. 32:28). Later, the nation of Israel was divided into two sections: the southern tribes of Judah and Benjamin, and the ten northern tribes. A *Jew* is literally a *physical* descendant from the tribe of Judah. An *Israelite* is a *physical* descendant from the ten northern tribes. However, in Ezekiel 37:16, God calls Judah as well as Ephraim (the ten northern tribes) "Israel."

Today the term *Jew* is used to identify all those who are the physical seed of Abraham through his son Isaac. Paul, who was from the tribe of Benjamin, called himself a Jew, an Israelite, and a Hebrew (see Acts 21:39; Rom. 11:1; Phil. 3:5), proving that all three terms are used interchangeably. Why did he call himself an Israelite if Israel was lost among the Gentiles? James also knew that they were in existence and not totally assimilated into the nations. He writes to them in James 1:1, saying, *"To the twelve tribes which are scattered abroad...."*

The terms *Jew* and *Israel* are used interchangeably throughout the New Covenant. Although the northern kingdom of Israel was destroyed in 749 B.C., representatives of all twelve tribes continued to live in the land of Israel, and all twelve tribes were called Israel.

Followers of the Two-House Theology love the Jewish people, but they take the spiritual truth of Jew and Gentile becoming One New Man too far. They are trying to *physically* become Israel, as though this would give them a special place in God's Kingdom. They are wrong. The special place in the Kingdom is being a child of God.

The Big Controversy

When a Christian looks at a Jew, he thinks, "I don't see anything Christian about you."

And when a Jew looks at a Christian, he thinks, "I don't see anything Jewish about you."

The rabbis say, "You can't be Jewish and believe in Jesus." Many Christians feel the same way.

How did the Jewish Messiah who was prophesied by the Jewish prophets in the Jewish Scriptures and who came "only" to the Jewish people (Matt. 15:24) become so Gentile? The first followers of Jesus were Jewish. The only Bible they had was the Jewish Scriptures. The first Church followed the biblical festivals, worshiped in the traditional synagogues, and was a sect within Judaism that believed Jesus was the Jewish Messiah.

The big controversy at the Jerusalem Council meeting in Acts 15:6-21 was over whether Gentiles had to become Jews to be saved. They do not. Today the big question is whether Jews have to become Gentiles to be saved. They do not.

The Jew First

The early Church, which was all Jewish, reached out to the Jew first. I call this the Law of Evangelism, which I will discuss in more detail in Chapter 10. God began this pattern by going to the first Jew, Abraham, in order to reach all the families on earth (see Gen. 12:3). Jesus instructed His first followers to go only *"to the lost sheep of the house of Israel"* (Matt. 10:5–6). Paul said in Romans 1:16, that the gospel is *"for the Jew first."* Although Paul was the apostle to the Gentiles, he always went first to the Jews. But, as the early Church spread into the non-Jewish world, it took on a more Gentile culture. Eventually, Gentiles outnumbered Jewish believers, and then the Jewish roots of the Church were removed.

Checkmate for the Devil

The restoration of the Jewish people to the body of Messiah is the key for worldwide revival. At the Jerusalem Council meeting in Acts 15, James quoted the prophet Amos: *"I will...rebuild the tabernacle of David...so that the rest of mankind may seek the Lord, even all the Gentiles who are called by My name..."* (Acts 15:16-17). The word *tabernacle* can be translated "house" or "family." What is Amos saying? When the family of David (the Jewish people) are restored (grafted back into their own olive tree), there will be revival among the Gentiles. And this will not be just any revival. Amos compared it to land producing crops so quickly that *"the plowman shall overtake the reaper"* (Amos 9:13). There has never been a time like this in history. The harvest of souls will be so great that church buildings will not be able to contain it.

Now you can understand the heart of God at this moment in history. Now you can see why so many Gentile Christians are interested in the Jewish roots of their faith. The Spirit of God is speaking this revelation to the Church worldwide. When the Jew is saved, not only will it open a supernatural door for large numbers of Gentiles to be saved, but it will also announce checkmate for the devil—the return of Jesus (see Matt. 23:39).

In order for the Jewish people to want what we (the Church) have, we must restore three key ingredients to Church life. The first is true intimacy with God. All services and ministry will flow out of this intimacy, not out of tradition. The second key is that all believers, even those with the smallest amount of faith, will move in the supernatural love and miracle-working power of God. The third key ingredient will be joyous celebrations of the biblical feasts. Adam enjoyed pure fellowship with God before sin brought separation and death. Jesus, the second Adam, came to restore that which was lost. God desires the same intimacy with us that He had with Adam before the Fall. He has even set appointments to meet with us.

My Appointments

God said in Leviticus 23:2, *"The **feasts** of the Lord, which you shall proclaim to be holy **convocations**, these are **My feasts**."* In Hebrew, the word translated *feasts* means "appointments," and the word translated *convocations* means "rehearsals." These appointments (feasts) with God are not only Jewish appointments, not only biblical appointments, but God also calls them *"My* appointments!"

There are seven specific appointments when God promises to meet with us. The first four were rehearsals of His First Coming and the outpouring of the Holy Spirit. I believe the next two are rehearsals of His Second Coming. The seventh, the Feast of Tabernacles, is a rehearsal of the millennial rule of Jesus on earth. If you had attended a dress rehearsal (convocation) of His First Coming before it happened, you would not have missed it. The same is true today. Celebrating the rehearsals (convocations) will help you prepare for His return.

In John's Gospel, 660 of the 879 verses are directly related to events occurring at the feasts. How can you understand the Gospels unless you understand the feasts? Of course, you should never let a religious spirit put you under bondage to these rehearsals. Observance is not a matter of righteousness or salvation, but of blessing. Isaiah 58:13-14 says that those who observe the Sabbath are promised to be so blessed that they will "ride on the high hills of the earth." Celebrating the feasts is not a "have to," but a "want to."

God tells us that when we bless the Jewish people we will be blessed in return (see Gen. 12:3). What greater way to do this than by inviting Jewish people to great celebrations where God promises in writing to meet with us? The reason God's glory will be released is because we will have such intimacy with Him as we yield completely to His Spirit. Every year our celebration of the festivals will be different. We will lay down our agenda for God's. (See Chapter 9 for ideas on how to celebrate the feasts.)

Prepare the Way

Paul wrote, *"The Jews require a sign* [miracle]*"* (1 Cor. 1:22 KJV). When we move into these God-appointed celebrations with Holy Spirit revelation and glory, miracles will take place, invoking jealousy in the Jews. Then the prayer of Jesus in John 17:21-22 will finally be answered. He prayed that the Jews and Gentiles would be one. The Jews will be grafted back into their own olive tree, and Jesus says that this combination of Jew and Gentile will cause the world to believe.

Jesus is not returning for a fractured, powerless Bride. As the Body of Messiah is restored, we will do the same works as Jesus and even *greater* (John 14:12). The *greater* works can only come when Jew and Gentile converge into One New Man. This supernatural unity of Jew and Gentile will prepare the way for the Lord. When the pattern is right, the glory will come down.

5

WHEN THE PATTERN
IS RIGHT...

I AM A JEW. Although as I was growing up I attended a traditional synagogue, it never dawned on me that I could know God personally. The stories about Moses, Noah, and Abraham belonged to another era. God seemed to be a million miles away—not relevant to my life. Even the most devout, older men in the synagogue were more interested in the ritualistic prayers and fellowship with their friends than in having an intimate relationship with God.

Today, most Jewish people are more secular than religious. When I was young, Jews at least went to the synagogue on high holidays like Rosh Hashanah and Yom Kippur. Now the majority of my people do not attend services at all.

When I encountered Jesus at the age of 30, everything in my world changed. I not only knew God was real, but I now knew Him personally. My biggest shock was to discover that Christians, for the most part, act like most Jews. They know about God. They believe in Him. They think they will probably go to Heaven. Yet some have greater intimacy with their denomination than with God. Others attend church merely for the social interaction. These Sunday and "high-holiday" (Easter and Christmas) Christians compartmentalize God according to their convenience. They treat Jesus more as their servant than as their Lord. They surrender Sunday mornings—not their lives.

Many churches have evolved into nothing more than religious warehouses filled with people bound for hell. Members are made to feel as if they are acceptable to God without repentance of sin. Their church experience is as spectators who never fulfill their destinies in God. Tragically, many do not even have a personal relationship with Jesus.

Over the years, I began to see that even some of the better churches are filled with religious tradition. The pastors appear to be more concerned with the offering, announcements, a full sermon, and a timely ending than with yielding to the leading of the Holy Spirit.

The more I hungered for greater intimacy with God, the more dissatisfied I became. Then God led me to study the history of the early Church. The blinders of tradition fell from my eyes. I began to see the Scriptures in a whole new light. Now I understand why there are so few miracles, even in believing, Spirit-filled churches. Now I know why so few believers fulfill their destiny in God. Now I know why the system forces the services to be man-controlled rather than God-controlled. Now I know why there is so little compassion for the souls of men and for the poor. Now I know why the sins of secular society pervade the Church. Now I know how we have grieved the Holy Spirit through ignorance, compromise, tradition, and the fear of man. Now I know why the glory under Moses was greater than our best churches today.

God has been waiting for a generation of believers to follow the cloud of His presence just as the Israelites followed the cloud in the wilderness. The cloud is moving. Will you follow the cloud to glory, or will you remain stuck in your old ways? Only a few of the older believers will enter this new land. The rest will observe it from afar. I am hungry for more. How about you?

Just as God had a specific plan for the Israelites to enter the Promised Land, He also instructed them on how to enter His glory. God said to Moses, *"See that you make all things according to the **pattern**..."* (Heb. 8:5). The pattern is God's bridge to intimacy. When the pattern is right, the glory explodes. Notice that I did not say *formula*, but *pattern*. Man wants to place God in a box, which is why we have so many religions and denominations. God is too big to be limited by our attempts to define Him. We cannot reduce His pattern to a formula. Formulas lead us to tradition, and tradition to fossilized, dead religion. The biblical pattern always leads to greater intimacy with God.

It also leads to unity between Jew and Gentile. I believe that today God is calling us to a new level in which both Jewish and Gentile believers will come together as One New Man—yielded to His Spirit and walking in power. *"For I am about to do something new. See, I have already begun"* (Isa. 43:19 NLT).

First the Natural, Then the Spiritual

God's pattern that defines the relationship between the Church and the Jewish people is explained in First Corinthians 15:46: *"The spiritual is not first, but the natural, and afterward the spiritual."* First, God acts with His natural people, Israel; then He acts with His spiritual people, the Church. His true Church is made up of those who genuinely believe in Jesus as Savior and Lord (both Jew and Gentile). The Church and Israel are *mishpochah*, which is Hebrew for "family." Whatever happens to Israel dramatically affects the restoration of the Church.

For example, in 1897 Theodor Herzl convened the first Zionist Congress in Basel, Switzerland, to investigate the formation of a Jewish homeland. The beginning of the restoration of the land birthed the beginning of the restoration of the manifest presence of the Holy Spirit in the Church. On New Year's Eve 1900, at a Bible school in Topeka, Kansas, a 30-year-old student named Agnes Ozman began to speak in tongues—the start of the Pentecostal Revival. Several days later, Charles Parham and other students also received the baptism of the Holy Spirit with the gift of speaking in tongues. After William Seymour sat under Parham's teaching, he took this fire to a home prayer meeting in Los Angeles that birthed the world-famous Azusa Street Revival.

Around the time when Israel became a nation in 1948, God responded by bringing the healing revival to the United States. Over 100 evangelists such as Oral Roberts, Kathryn Kuhlman, T.L. Osborn, and Kenneth Hagin began tremendous healing ministries. Billy Graham's ministry also started then.

In 1967, Israel regained possession of Jerusalem for the first time since the temple was destroyed. That same year, the Catholic Charismatic movement started. It went on to impact Christians from all denominations. The late 1960s also gave birth to the Jesus Movement, which swept thousands of hippies into the Kingdom of God.

Around the time of the Yom Kippur War in 1973, revival broke out among Jewish people, resulting in the modern-day Messianic Jewish movement.

What's Next?

If you want to know what the next move of God will be—watch Israel. Because of sin, God scattered the Jewish people to the four corners of the earth. But in the last days He promises to restore them to Israel. (See Ezekiel 37:21.) In the Old Covenant, the nation of Israel was a divided land. The northern kingdom was called Israel, and the southern kingdom, Judah. Judah and Israel fought with each other. God promises to restore these two kingdoms and to return them to their land. They will be one nation under one King:

> *And I will make them one nation in the land, on the mountains of Israel; and one king shall be king over them all; they shall no longer be two nations, nor shall they ever be divided into two kingdoms again* (Ezekiel 37:22).

Today we are seeing these Scriptures fulfilled before our eyes. Israel is a nation again, and the Jews are returning to Israel in record numbers. A sign of the hastening of the prophetic time clock is when the Jews from the north of Israel (from the former Soviet Union) return to the land. Jeremiah 16:14-16 says that once this happens, Jews from the entire world will return to Israel.

We are also beginning to see the spiritual fulfill-ment of Ezekiel's prophecy. The two covenant peoples of God, Jews and Christians, who have been divided for centuries, will unite under one King—Jesus. This will cause a spiritual explosion in the Church. The devil's worst nightmare will come to pass when the sleeping giant, the Church, finally realizes that the underlying purpose for the current outpourings of the Holy Spirit is to equip believers with power to evangelize the Jew. When the Jewish people join with the Gentiles to form One New Man, it will trigger a major release of power to evangelize the world. But before the Church can enter this glorious future, it must first overcome its anti-Semitic past.

6

CHRISTIAN?

GOD HAS A MARVELOUS PLAN for bringing about the unity of the Jew and the Gentile in Messiah Jesus. The apostle Paul wrote, *"To provoke* [the Jews] *to jealousy, salvation has come to the Gentiles"* (Rom. 11:11). God wants to use Gentiles to bring the Jewish people back into the Body of Messiah. Somehow that truth has gotten lost. To provoke the Jew to jealousy means to demonstrate the supernatural peace, healing, strong family relationships, and love that only come from intimacy with God. It means causing the Jew to want what Gentile believers have.

Instead of driving the Jewish people to jealousy, the Christian Church has simply driven them away. Although there are believers who have given their lives for the Jews,[1] some of the most anti-Jewish people in the last two thousand years have been those who have called themselves Christians. Through the centuries, Church leaders' accusations and statements against the

Jews have led to a vicious form of "Christian" anti-Semitism. Here are a few examples:[2]

- Justin Martyr (d. A.D. 167) was one of the first to accuse the Jews of inciting to kill Christians.

- Origen (d. A.D. 254) accused Jews of plotting in their meetings to murder Christians.

- Eusebius (c. A.D. 300) alleged that Jews engaged in ceremonial killing of Christian children each year at the holiday of Purim.

- St. Hilary of Poitiers (d. A.D. 367) said that the Jews were a perverse people, forever accursed by God.

- St. Ephraem (d. A.D. 373) wrote many of the early church hymns, some of which maligned Jews, even to the point of calling the Jewish synagogues "whore houses."

- St. John Chrysostom (A.D. 344–407) said that there could never be expiation for the Jews and that God had always hated them. He said it was "incumbent" upon all Christians to hate the Jews; they were assassins of Christ, and worshipers of the devil. In one of his homilies, Chrysostom stated: "The synagogue is worse than a brothel....It is a den of scoundrels and the repair of wild beasts...the temple of demons devoted to idolatrous cults...the refuge of brigands and debauchees, and the cavern of devils."[3]

- St. Cyril (d. A.D. 444) gave the Jews within his jurisdiction the choice of conversion, exile, or stoning.

- St. Jerome (d. A.D. 420), translator of the Latin Vulgate, "proved" that Jews are incapable of understanding the Scriptures and said they should be severely persecuted until they confess the "true faith."

- St. Augustine (d. A.D. 430) said the true image of the Jew was Judas Iscariot, forever guilty and spiritually ignorant. St. Augustine decided that Jews, for their own good and the good of society, must be relegated to the position of slaves. This theme was later picked up by St. Thomas Aquinas (d. A.D. 1274), who demanded that Jews be called to perpetual servitude. According to Professor F.E. Talmage, St. Augustine believed that "because of their sin against Christ, the Jews rightly deserved death. Yet, as with Cain who murdered the just Abel, they are not to die....For they are doomed to wander the earth...the 'witnesses of their iniquity and of our truth,' the living proof of Christianity."[4]

- The Crusaders (A.D. 1099) herded Jews into the Great Synagogue in Jerusalem. When they were securely inside the locked doors, the synagogue was set on fire. And the misguided Crusaders, with the lies of perverted sermons fresh in their ears, sang as they marched around the blaze, "Christ, we adore Thee."

- Martin Luther (c. A.D. 1544) said the Jews should not merely be slaves, but slaves of slaves and that they might not even come into contact with Christians. In his *Schem Hamphoras*, he said the Jews were ritual murderers and poisoners of wells. He called for all Talmuds and synagogues to be destroyed. In his *Von den Juden und Iren Luegen* (1543), Luther wrote: "What then shall we Christians do with this damned, rejected race of Jews? Since they live among us and we know about their lying and blasphemy and cursing, we cannot tolerate them if we do not wish to share in their lies, curses, and blasphemy....We must prayerfully and reverentially practice a merciful severity."[5] *Encyclopaedia Judaica* comments on Luther's statements: "Short of the Auschwitz oven and extermination, the whole Nazi Holocaust is pre-outlined here."[6] Indeed, Adolph Hitler wrote in *Mein Kampf*, "Hence today I believe that I am acting in accordance with the Almighty Creator: by defending myself against the Jew, I am fighting for the work of the Lord."[7]

Speaking as part of the Church, we need a restoration miracle. Only God can restore the damage between the Church and the Jewish people. Repentance is the first step. We may not have been knowingly anti-Semitic, but as members of His Body, we must repent for the sins of the whole Church. Daniel did not rebel against God, but he repented on behalf of Israel. Some feel we should not talk of this sad history. How then can we ever repent and get clean?[8] The Church must be rid of this horrible sin. Otherwise, without holiness, we will not see God (see Heb. 12:14). Step one toward maturity involves repentance. Thank God for the Passover Lamb who takes away the sins of the whole world.

7

THE CONSTANTINE CONSPIRACY

CAN A BELIEVER be under a curse for the anti-Semitic attitudes of his ancestors? Just ask Eric Carlson. While serving as a submarine officer, Eric had a life-changing visitation from God that lasted for three days. The Lord revealed to him that he was Jewish. Eric later discovered that his grandfather had changed his last name when he immigrated to America in order to hide his Jewish identity. Then God told Eric he was under a family curse for denying his Jewish heritage and that the curse had to be broken. After he prayed to break the curse, Eric was flooded with revelation and blessings. Today Eric is a Messianic Jewish rabbi of a One New Man congregation. (See Eric's teaching on celebrating the feasts in Chapter 9.)

God says He will bless those who bless the Jewish people and curse those who curse them (see Gen. 12:3).

Mixture in God's House

Could the Church be under a family curse just as Eric was? Has the Church denied its Jewish heritage? Yes. As we saw in the previous chapter, anti-Semitism has been a prominent part of Church history for centuries. This was not an accident. It was part of a deliberate plan to separate the Church from anything Jewish. Let's call it what it was—a conspiracy.

The first Church was Jewish. If a Gentile wanted to follow the Messiah, he had to convert to Judaism. Then Peter had a revelation that Gentiles did not have to convert to Judaism to be saved (see Acts 10). The Jerusalem Council meeting determined that Gentiles did not have to be circumcised. There were only four easily followed requirements. They were to *"abstain from things polluted by idols, from sexual immorality, from things strangled, and from blood"* (Acts 15:20). After all, James said, they could learn more about God by hearing the words of Moses every Saturday in the synagogue (see Acts 15:21). This opened the door to widespread church growth among the Gentiles. So many Gentiles were saved that the Jewish believers became a minority.

The first Jewish followers of Jesus were called "Nazarenes" (part of the Essenes sect of Judaism discussed in Chapter 3). They practiced traditional Judaism and were widely accepted by unbelieving Jews. Early in the second century their numbers reached

400,000.[1] In the Book of Acts, the early church fathers said to Paul: *"You see, brother, how many myriads* [tens of thousands] *of Jews there are who have believed, and they are all zealous for the law"* (Acts 21:20).

The Nazarenes' acceptance by traditional Jews came to a halt in A.D. 135 when Rabbi Akiba declared that Bar Kochba was the Jewish Messiah. His followers hoped he would lead them to victory over the Romans. The Nazarenes refused to fight because they believed Jesus was the true Messiah rather than Bar Kochba. They were branded traitors, not because they believed in Jesus, but because they would not join Bar Kochba's armed struggle. Bar Kochba and his followers were quickly slaughtered by the Romans. Afterward, Jews were banned from Jerusalem.

History shows that as the center of the Christian faith moved from Jerusalem to Rome, it became increasingly Hellenized, adopting pagan customs and philosophies rather than the God-ordained practices and beliefs of the Bible. At the same time, Christianity became increasingly anti-Jewish.

In the early fourth century (A.D. 306–337), the Roman emperor Constantine, came into power. He was a master politician. He tried to attract heathens to Christianity by modifying pagan customs and festivals and giving them Christian meanings, which would still allow the Christians to keep their traditions. But he

didn't like the Jews since they had rebelled against
Rome. And the Church was more than willing to follow Constantine's lead in order to avoid persecution.
Christians were prohibited from worshiping on
Saturday or observing Passover, upon the threat of
excommunication or worse. Constantine expressed the
anti-Judaic sentiments of the bishops of the Christian
world when he wrote:

> *Let us therefore have nothing in common with
> this odious people, the Jews, for we have received from
> our Savior a different way.... Strive and pray con-
> tinually that the purity of your souls may not be sul-
> lied by fellowship with the customs of these most
> wicked men.... All should unite in desiring that
> which sound reason appears to demand in avoiding all
> participation in the perjured conduct of the Jews.[2]*

In A.D. 196, without the presence of Jewish believers, a church council meeting in Caesarea changed the
celebration of Jesus' resurrection from the third day of
Passover [First fruits] (see Lev. 23:9–11; 1 Cor. 15:
4;20–23) to Sunday, during the feast of the pagan fertility goddess, Ishtar. In the fourth century, the
Council of Nicea (headed by Constantine) made the
change official. The decision was based on the premise
that it was not proper for the Church's celebrations to
be connected with "the cursed Jewish nation" that

crucified Christ.[3] Today, the holiday is known as Easter (from Ishtar).

Have you ever wondered why we have Easter bunnies and eggs? These are vestiges of Ishtar worship. The prejudice was so strong that the translators of the King James Bible intentionally mistranslated the Greek word that means "Passover" as *Easter* (see Acts 12:4, KJV). This mistranslation is found in King James Bibles even today!

Too Cold

Another major change that started early in Church history was the celebration of Christmas. Today it is the most hallowed religious holiday next to Easter. But was Jesus born on December 25? According to Luke 2:8, we know He was not. Shepherds would not have been out in the field watching their flocks *at night* in Bethlehem in December because it would have been too cold.

It makes more sense that Jesus would have been born about the time of Sukkot (Feast of Tabernacles). This feast is referred to as "the Season of Our Joy." What greater joy than for the Messiah to tabernacle— or dwell—with man? Scripture tells us that the law, which includes biblical festivals, is a *"shadow of the good things to come"* (Heb. 10:1). Sukkot foreshadows the dwelling of God with man. *"And the Word became flesh* *and **dwelt*** [tabernacled] *among us*" (John 1:14). The Feast of Tabernacles provides a much better picture of Jesus than Christmas.

So where did the idea of celebrating the birth of Jesus on December 25 originate? Babylonian pagans believed the sun was god. The winter solstice began on December 21 and represented the death of the sun. By December 25, a wild celebration of the sun's "rebirth" took place. This rebirth celebration was in honor of the incarnation of the sun god and his mother, the "queen of heaven." To draw pagans into Christianity, the Roman Catholic Church proclaimed December 25 to be the birthday of the Messiah, although this is not mentioned in Scripture. The festival was called Christ's Masse and was later shortened to Christmas.[4] The early Puritans knew this history and, therefore, did not celebrate Christmas.[5]

Whatever Happened to the Sabbath?

Another reform by the Council of Nicea institutionalized the change of the day of Christian worship from Saturday to Sunday. As with Easter, the change had actually started much earlier. In fact, by the middle of the second century, Sunday, the day devoted to the sun god, had largely replaced Saturday, the day devoted to the one true God. The Sabbath was the first element of Creation that God sanctified, or set apart, in remembrance of His creative power. That God rested on the Sabbath day is a biblical fact. Nevertheless, the change was made and justified by the Church leaders, and not initially on the basis of the Resurrection. The primary rationale for the observance of Sunday was to commemorate the first day of Creation. The resurrection of Jesus was only a secondary issue.

Many of the church leaders who originally changed the Sabbath day were anti-Semitic. Tertullian thought that God had always hated the Sabbath.[6] The Epistle of Barnabas (apocryphal literature from the first century A.D.) denies altogether that God had ever given the Sabbath as a commandment to be kept. Justin Martyr (d. A.D. 167) considered the Sabbath to be a highly deserved curse on the Jewish people. Martyr lectured Trypho the Jew by saying, "It was by reason of your sins and the sins of your Fathers that, among other precepts, God imposed upon you the observance of the Sabbath as a mark." This "mark" was to "single them out for the punishment they so well deserved for their infidelities."[7]

Instead of recognizing that *"the Sabbath was made for man"* (Mark 2:27), the Church saw the Sabbath as part of the curse of the law upon that hated and despised race—the Jews. The post-apostolic Church instituted another day of worship to separate themselves from all things Jewish. This anti-Judaism was reflected in the Replacement Theology of the early writers of the Hellenized Church. (See Chapter 4 for a discussion of Replacement Theology.)

Where's the Power?

It is no coincidence that when the Jewish biblical heritage of the Church was replaced with paganism, intimacy with God was watered down. The Church went from everyone doing the works of Jesus to professional clergy leading a congregation of spectators. The supernatural power of God was replaced with the politics and traditions of men.[8] Jesus warned against this when He rebuked the religious leaders of His day for *"making the Word of God of no effect through your tradition"* (Mark 7:13).

When the Church walked away from its biblical Jewish roots, it abandoned God's pattern. The original Church split was the division between Jew and Gentile. When the Jewish believers and Gentile believers come together in Jesus, we will break the curse off of the Church and clear the way for widespread revival.

8

BIBLICAL FESTIVALS— BLESSING OR BONDAGE?

THE BIGGEST LIE THE DEVIL TELLS Jewish people is that they can't be Jewish and believe in Jesus. By hiding its Jewish roots, the Church has reinforced this lie. Isn't it time that the Body of Messiah become mature and start to look like the Jewish olive tree? Now is the time for Jewish believers and Christians alike to see Christianity's Jewish connection and celebrate this union. Part of the Church's heritage is to observe the biblical festivals as God meant them to be observed. As a means of reinforcing the unity of the two streams into one, I will refer to Jesus by His Hebrew name, Yeshua, for the remainder of the book.

Under the Law?

The first church observed all the biblical festivals. During the Millennium (the thousand-year reign of Yeshua on earth) we will observe the Sabbath, the Feast of Tabernacles, Rosh Hashanah (the Feast of

Trumpets), the Passover, and the Feast of Unleavened Bread (see Isa. 66:23; Zech. 14:16–17; Ezek. 45:20–21). Why have we put these celebrations on hold for centuries?

One reason is that many resist anything that appears to put them under the law. The Hebrew word translated "law" is *torah* and should have been translated "instructions." Paul makes it clear that we are not justified by the instructions (see Rom. 3:20; Eph. 2:8–9). Does this mean that the instructions have no value? Should we disregard such instructions as the Ten Commandments? Of course not. Paul proclaimed, *"Therefore the law* [instructions] *is holy, and the commandment holy and just and good"* (Rom. 7:12).

Yeshua explained this paradox in Matthew 5:18: *"Till Heaven and earth pass away, one jot or one tittle will by no means pass from the law* [instructions] *till all is fulfilled."* The key word in this passage is *fulfilled.* This word is best understood by reversing the syllables of *ful-filled* to *filled-full.* Yeshua is the full meaning of the law. He did not come to eliminate the instructions but to enable us to fill them full of their true meaning.

Yeshua was never upset with the instructions. He said, *"Do not think that I came to destroy the Law* [instructions] *or the Prophets. I did not come to destroy but to fulfill"* (Matt. 5:17). What He did object to were the ways in which the rabbis would cleverly overrule many portions of the instructions. Yeshua asked, *"Why do you also transgress the commandment of God because of your tradition?"* (Matt. 15:3).

Before you conclude that I am advocating a new form of bondage or legalism, let's get one thing straight. Celebrating the Jewish biblical feasts has nothing to do with obtaining salvation or righteousness. This was the mistake of the Judaizers in the Book of Galatians. It is only through repentance of our sins and the blood of Yeshua that we are saved. Nothing more is needed. However, observing the festivals does bring blessing and leads to greater intimacy with God. (See Chapter 9 for an overview of the feasts and how a One New Man congregation celebrates them.)

Appointed Times

So what should be our attitude toward the biblical feasts? The Hebrew word for *feasts* is *mo'ed*, which means "appointed times." Leviticus 23:2 makes it clear that these are not only Jewish feasts, but they are *God's* feasts. In other words, these are God's appointed times to meet with us. Would you ignore or arrive late for your set time to meet with the president of your country? It may not cost you your life, but you would miss a great honor and blessing. How much more of a blessing will you miss if you stand-up God at His set appointments? God calls the feasts "convocations," which in the Hebrew means "rehearsals" (Lev. 23:2).

> *Speak unto the children of Israel, and say unto them, Concerning the feasts of the Lord, which ye shall proclaim to be holy* **convocations**, *even these are My feasts* (Leviticus 23:2, KJV).

God says we should observe these rehearsals at His appointed times *forever* (see Lev. 16:29; 23:14, 21, 31, 41). Since the festivals were such clear shadows of Yeshua's First Coming, they must hold significant keys to His return. How would you like to attend a dress rehearsal of the return of Messiah? Colossians 2:16-17 shows us that festivals and sabbaths *"are a shadow of things to come."* How can we celebrate great events in God's history or have revelation of His return if we throw out the set appointments?

Instead of seeing the New Covenant as being disconnected from the Old, a better way to describe it is as the *Renewed* Covenant. According to Bible scholar William Morford, one of the definitions of the Hebrew word for *new* in Jeremiah 31:31 is "renewed." When this verse is quoted in Hebrews 8:8, the Greek word used for *new* can also be defined as "renewed." Yeshua said, *"Do not think that I came to annul, to bring an incorrect interpretation to, the Torah or the Prophets: I did not come to annul but to bring spiritual abundance."* (Matt. 5:17 PNT).

We should observe (fulfill) the feasts as great, spiritually abundant freedom celebrations. It is as if God is throwing a party and inviting us to attend. We will observe these festivals in the Millennium (see Isa. 66:23; Zech. 14:16). So much revelation about Yeshua is ready to be released as we worship God at these appointed times.

Passover

For example, the Passover dinner gives us insight about the last days. The first New Covenant Passover was actually an engagement dinner. It was not just a reminder of the Exodus from Egypt, but it was a promise of a future exodus from earth. In ancient Judaism, an engagement was as binding as a marriage. After the engagement, the bridegroom went to prepare a room in his father's house for his bride.

At the Last Supper, Yeshua drank the third cup of wine—"the cup of redemption," which He called the *"new covenant in my blood"* (Luke 22:20).[1] In the context of the marriage customs of ancient Israel, He was also making a kind of betrothal statement. Earlier, He had told His disciples, *"I go to prepare a place for you. And if I go and prepare a place for you, I will come again and receive you to Myself; that where I am, there you may be also"* (John 14:2-3).

The custom in those days was for a bridegroom to pay a dowry, either in goods or services, to the father of his bride as compensation for the loss of her presence in their household. In drinking the cup of redemption, Yeshua was saying to His Bride, the Church, "I will redeem you—I will pay the price for you." Yeshua's blood on the cross was the highest price ever paid for a bride. It released the Holy Spirit to assemble this new Bride, made up of Jews and Gentiles who become One New Man in Yeshua.

The fourth cup of wine that we drink at the Passover meal is called "the cup of praise." Yeshua did not drink this cup on earth. After the third cup, He said, *"But I say to you, I will not drink of this fruit of the vine from now on until that day when I drink it new with you in My Father's kingdom"* (Matt. 26:29). That day will come when the Church, the Bride, the One New Man, is caught up in the air to be with Yeshua (see 1 Thess. 4:16-17). We will share with Him in the marriage supper of the Lamb—a heavenly Passover meal (see Rev. 19:7-9).

Blessing, Not Bondage

As a traditional Jew, I used to follow the festivals the same way each year. Eventually, I got bored with traditions learned by rote. When I became a Messianic Jew, I found hidden meanings about the Messiah in the festivals. I saw purpose in the celebrations. But observing the same events in exactly the same way—year after year—became boring again. For me, it became more of a form of entertainment, or tradition, rather than a spiritual encounter with God.

So what is the answer? We should not necessarily follow the Rabbinic interpretations and traditions or even our new Messianic understandings exactly the same way every time. Instead of being traditional about how we observe the festivals, we should study each festival in the Scriptures. Then pray, "Holy Spirit, how can we glorify Yeshua in a special way at this appointed time?"

Yeshua performed more miracles on the Sabbath than on any other day. I have found that God increases the anointing for miracles and evangelism during the festivals. When you celebrate these feasts, you know that God is pleased. I believe that there are supernatural blessings connected with observing the biblical festivals in liberty. For instance, God specifically promises those who observe the Sabbath: *"I will give you great honor and give you your full share of the inheritance I promised to Jacob, your ancestor. I, the Lord, have spoken"* (Isa. 58:14 NLT).

Churches are beginning to use the seven biblical festivals (Passover, Unleavened Bread, First Fruits, Pentecost, Trumpets, Day of Atonement, and Tabernacles) as corporate worship events. We are also told to teach the festivals to our children (see Exod. 12:26-27). I believe God would be honored if we set the Sabbath apart for family time. Because of His supernatural promises, God will use this time to restore families. This is a great way for Yeshua to fulfill (fill full of Himself) the fourth commandment.

Unholy Merger

Prophets such as Jeremiah and Hosea forbade the Jewish people to merge paganism with belief in God. (See Jeremiah 7:30-31; Hosea 3:1.) Jeremiah 2:13 says that the people had committed two evils: they had forsaken God's vessel and they had made their own defective vessels.

> *For My people have committed two evils; they have forsaken Me the fountain of living waters, and hewed them out cisterns, broken cisterns, that can hold no water* (Jer. 2:13 KJV).

In the early church, Jewish believers in the Messiah were forced by Gentile Christians to give up worship on the Sabbath and other biblical festivals under threat of excommunication or death. As we saw in the previous chapter, these godly shadows and prophetic pictures of the Messiah's First Coming, His return, and the millennial reign were replaced with pagan traditions.

What are we to do today? Are we to give up Sunday worship? Not necessarily. The key is not that we should abandon Sunday as a day of worship, but that we should repent of the anti-Semitic attitudes of the early Church leaders who established Sunday worship.

Does the Bible tell us to worship on Sunday? No. The Bible mentions that some gathered on the first day of the week. One reason for this was because tithes, alms giving, and business of any kind could not be conducted on the Sabbath. Nowhere in Scripture are we *commanded* to worship on Sunday.

Many refer to Sunday as "the Lord's day," giving it special significance as a holy day. What is the Lord's day? Psalm 118:24 says, "***This*** *is the day which the Lord has made; we will rejoice and be glad in it.*" Today most Christians worship the Lord on Sunday. But God has selected *every* day to be the day the Lord has made or the "Lord's day." Since Sunday is usually a day we do not have to work, it is a convenient time for corporate worship. However, that doesn't make it the Sabbath.

Celebrating in Joy and Freedom

Hosea 3:4–5 says:

> *For the children of Israel shall abide many days with-*
> *out king or prince, without sacrifice or sacred pillar,*
> *without ephod or teraphim. Afterward the children of*
> *Israel shall return and seek the Lord their God and*
> *David their king.*

In other words, in the latter days there will be a revival among the Jewish people. This is the set time to favor Zion (Israel). (See Psalm 102:13.) True repentance, or change in behavior, by the Church will release this Jewish revival. What would demonstrate true repentance on behalf of the Christians for the anti-Semitism of the Church and the persecution that forced Jewish believers to reject their biblical festivals? Reconciliation meetings have been a good start, but we need to go deeper. Not much has changed. Israel is not saved. What about repenting by restoring the Jewish roots of the faith?

Some congregations will worship only on the Sabbath, which is also known as the *Shabbat*. The biblical Shabbat begins on Friday evening at sundown. Other congregations will worship on Shabbat and Sunday. Instead of a Sunday morning service and a Sunday evening service, how about a Friday evening and a Sunday morning service? Others will take

Saturday as a true day of rest, a family day. At this time, this is how I personally observe Shabbat. The feasts of the Lord are for Him. He says, *"These are My feasts"* (Lev. 23:2). But the Sabbath was made for man to rest. *"The Sabbath was made for man, and not man for the Sabbath"* (Mark 2:27).

Several years ago, I attended a teaching meeting and met a woman who had little joy. When I told her I was Jewish, her countenance brightened. She told me that she attended a church that worshiped on the Sabbath, but was spiritually dead. She wanted to go to another church that was alive in the Spirit, but it met on Sunday. When I suggested she go to both, she said, "I don't have the time, so I must go to the one that allows me to celebrate the true Sabbath."

I asked her, "Where in the Bible does it command you to attend church on Saturday?" She could not answer. Then I recommended she take Saturday to be with her family at home as a day of rest. I could see a heavy weight lift off of her as she saw freedom for the first time.

I am not suggesting a rigid tradition. Pray about it, and do what is pleasing to God. Do not make the Shabbat a legalistic formula. At the same time, do not act as if Sunday worship is a legalistic formula. Never lose sight of the objective. The objective is not Jewish roots, but the Jewish Messiah, who is our Sabbath.

Let me warn you by saying that this is not another segmented ministry of the Church such as a singles group or just another meeting like Wednesday night prayer. If that is how you view the Sabbath, then you have missed the Spirit of God. The idea behind a Shabbat service is for the congregation to totally identify with its biblical roots and with the Jewish people and the Jewish Messiah. If the majority attend on Sunday and just a few on Shabbat, you will end up with two congregations. God is after One New Man, not a few segregated events.

Some will take the revelation of Jewish roots and create a legalistic system based on a works mentality. Eventually, these Judaizers will evolve into a denomination and fossilize. A religious spirit will settle on them. Their identity will be in their Jewish culture rather than in the Jewish Messiah. They will cause much disunity in the Body. Many in the Church will fight this religious Jewish roots movement because of the legalists.

Others in the Jewish roots movement will completely divorce themselves from the Gentile Church and embrace elements of Rabbinic Judaism. Sadly, the anti-Christ spirit of traditional rabbis who deny the deity of Yeshua will infect some. The supernatural allure of man-made tradition attracts these religious spirits. Their ultimate assignment is to make the believer convert to traditional Rabbinic Judaism and renounce Yeshua.

Those same religious spirits can attach themselves to extra-biblical traditions within Christianity. These spirits try to convince the believer that the Church has replaced the Jew and Israel. (See Chapter 4.) This anti-Semitic stance opens the door to other heresies.

The devil tries to get us in a religious ditch on one side of the road or the other—either "Christian" anti-Semitism or Judaism without Yeshua. But a new move of God's Spirit will blow on the Church, and a new freedom in biblical festivals will come forth.

9

CELEBRATE THE FEASTS

IN THIS CHAPTER, my friend Dr. John Fischer, a Jewish believer in Yeshua, gives his overview of the biblical and spiritual meaning of all the festivals.[1] After the description of each feast, my friend Rabbi Eric Carlson, leader of a One New Man congregation, explains how his congregation celebrates these feasts. The sections labeled "Overview of..." were written by Dr. Fischer. Rabbi Carlson wrote the sections labeled "How to Celebrate...."

These celebrations come to life when they are filled with the Spirit of God, when His Spirit shows you how He wants you to observe them every year. No more "same-old, same-old." Expect a visitation from God.

Overview of Passover Week

Pesach

Exodus 12 and the earlier chapters tell the story of Pesach (Passover). Nine plagues had not convinced

Egypt's Pharaoh to release the Jewish people. God had one final plague in mind. In order to be protected from this plague, each Jewish family had to kill a lamb and apply its blood to the door of their home. When the angel of destruction passed through Egypt, he "passed over" the homes that had the lamb's blood on the door.

Traditionally, Pesach is observed much as it has been since before Yeshua. The major exceptions include the presence of the lamb bone replacing the eating of the lamb and the addition of the *Afikomen* (It is *matzoh*, unleavened bread, made of plain flour and water that is hidden and served as a "dessert" at this meal.)[2]

An incident from the time of the second temple highlights the Messianic significance of Pesach. At that time people traveled great distances to observe the holiday in Jerusalem. They would then go to the temple area to select a lamb for the festival. There the priest would indicate an appropriate lamb by pointing to the animal and saying, "Behold the lamb." On one occasion John the Baptist, the son of a priest, saw Yeshua coming in the distance, pointed, and said, *"Behold, the Lamb...."* But he went on to complete his statement, *"...of God, who takes away the sin of the world"* (John 1:29 NIV). He thus indicated that Yeshua's forthcoming sacrificial death was related to the meaning of Pesach. Later, the apostle Paul stated, *"For [Messiah], our Passover lamb, has been sacrificed"* (1 Cor. 5:7 NIV).

Yeshua, the Messiah, acted as God's Passover lamb for us; He died that we might live. Before He died, Yeshua took one of the cups of wine during Pesach and said that it represented His blood, which would shortly be shed on our behalf for the forgiveness of sins. (See Matthew 26:27-28.) This would have reminded His followers of the blood of the Passover lamb that was applied to the doorposts in Egypt.

Now, as we celebrate Pesach, we remember not only God's actions during the time of the Exodus but also Yeshua's death for us, which secured our atonement. In fact, the term used for the piece of matzoh that is "hidden" during the Pesach meal, *Afikomen*—a Greek, not Hebrew, term—literally means "the one who came." It was used in the first couple of centuries as a title of Yeshua the Messiah.[3]

Feast of Unleavened Bread

Leviticus 23:6-8 describes this festival, which is closely connected to Pesach and also uses unleavened bread. Unleavened bread (matzoh) may well picture pure bread in that it has no yeast-like agents. In this sense it remains uncontaminated. For this reason, leaven frequently represented evil (see 1 Cor. 5:6–7). This feast became part of the Passover week observance because of the command to eat matzoh for seven days during Pesach (see Exod. 12:18).

When Yeshua ate His last Passover meal, He took the matzoh, broke it—as we do even today—and said it represented His body, which would be given as a sacrifice for us (see Matt. 26:26), hence, the significance of "pure" or unleavened bread.

Ceremony of First fruits

According to Leviticus 23:9-14, the ceremony of first fruits occurs immediately after Pesach. The very first part of the harvest is waved before God, a symbolic way of presenting it to God, *"so it will be accepted on your behalf"* (Lev. 23:11 NIV). Traditional observance associates this ceremony with Passover week. The beginning of the 50-day period of counting the omer (counting the days between Passover and Shavuot), which is observed by traditional Jews, reflects this ceremony today.

Three days after His death and right after Pesach, Yeshua rose from the dead (see Matt. 28:1-10). The apostle Paul wrote that by rising from the dead, Yeshua became *"...the **firstfruits** of those who have fallen asleep* [died]*"* (1 Cor. 15:20 NIV). Like the first fruits in Leviticus 23:11, His resurrection was *"accepted for us"* as He was *"raised...for our justification"* (Rom. 4:25 NIV). So the ceremony of the first fruits and its traditional counterpart, the beginning of the counting of the omer, should remind us of Yeshua's resurrection. The resurrection demonstrated that He was indeed the

Messiah and that His sacrifice had in fact secured atonement for us.

As we recall the significance of Passover week, we recognize several truths. The blood of the Passover lamb reminds us of Yeshua's great loss of blood at His crucifixion, and the matzoh recalls His body sacrificed on our behalf. These holidays picture His death. The ceremony of first fruits pictures His resurrection. Thus, the Messianic significance of Passover week relates to the atonement made for us by Yeshua the Messiah, effected by His death and resurrection.

How to Celebrate Pesach (Passover)

When feast days approach, the first things we do as a One New Man congregation are pray, fast, and seek God's guidance through the Holy Spirit on how to celebrate. We could perform the traditional liturgical celebration, but we prefer serving God and His will *today*. He desires us to have celebrations where life abounds and He is present. It is nothing short of supernatural how strongly the Holy Spirit works if we step aside and let Him move freely. Feast-day celebrations bring revival (see 2 Chron. 30). The hardest aspect to overcome in the flesh (especially for pastors) is to step aside and let God and the Holy Spirit work. We must humbly submit ourselves to God in truth and love so that the Holy Spirit can move freely.

When we pray and submit ourselves to God and ask what to do, He always answers, *always*! Here are a few Passover examples of what the Holy Spirit has led us to do in previous years. I am not saying you should celebrate the same way we do, and I am not saying you should not. I am merely giving examples of how the Spirit leads us as a congregation and giving you something to pray and think about.

One year we wrote a short play telling the Passover story. At the conclusion of the play, we circulated Communion elements—matzoh and grape juice—and held Communion. That year six Orthodox Jews who saw the Jewish Messiah in this play partook of Communion with us and accepted Yeshua. Another year we used a rough outline of a traditional *Seder* (order of service). We placed a Seder plate on every table with the various items, matzoh, and grape juice. Using the items on the Seder plate as symbols, we taught how sin is bondage and how we have been delivered from the bondage of sin by the Perfect Lamb, Yeshua. We then took the matzoh and juice, had Communion, and worshiped in music and dance for several hours. That year we witnessed several healing miracles as the presence of the Lord descended upon us while we worshiped and praised the living God.

Another time the Holy Spirit directed us to invite a prominent worship leader. We had a catered meal and retold the story of the Exodus from Egypt. The children searched our hall for a hidden piece of leavened bread, learning that leavening is like sin and that we must search ourselves diligently to root out all the sin in our lives. We then had Communion. Afterward the worship leader led us in worship (song and dance) for several hours. People were supernaturally healed, and two people received Yeshua that night as their personal Savior. All we did was worship the God of Israel as He commanded us to do. I have also used items from the traditional Passover Seder to teach school groups how Yeshua was and is prophetically foreshadowed throughout Scripture.

Overview of Shavuot

Chronologically, Shavuot (Pentecost), the Feast of Weeks, occurs next in the original Jewish calendar (see Lev. 23:15-22). This special time takes place 50 days after the first fruits ceremony. Along with other offerings, two loaves of leavened bread were presented to God. Deuteronomy 16:9-17 indicates that, although this festival accompanied the harvest, it was intended to remind us that we were once slaves in Egypt before God set us free.

As our traditions developed, Shavuot became the festival of the giving of the Law. Evidently, the rabbis concluded by calculations that the giving of the Law at Mt. Sinai took place on this day. Traditional Jews read the scroll of Ruth in the synagogue on this day and occasionally refer to Shavuot as *Atzeret shel Pesach*, "the completion of Passover." Messianic significance abounds in this festival. From God's perspective, the time of great harvest—when large numbers of Jews and then Gentiles came into a personal relationship with Him—was initiated at the Shavuot after Yeshua's resurrection (see Acts 2:40-43). The two leavened (impure) loaves of Shavuot *may* therefore symbolize Jew and Gentile, which are presented to God and are now part of His family.

The apostle Paul's teaching about our former conditions as slaves to sin (see Rom. 6–8) is certainly reminiscent of Shavuot's reminder that we were formerly slaves in Egypt. God set us free from slavery to sin by placing His Spirit in us to enable us to live as He intended (see Rom. 8:1-4). God visibly placed His Spirit (*Ruach HaKodesh*) in Yeshua's followers on that important Shavuot centuries ago (see Acts 2:4).

Technically, the work of atonement is not complete unless man's sin nature (*yetzer hara*, which translates "evil inclination") has been dealt with, and the power to overcome it has been granted. The coming of the Ruach HaKodesh served as the completion of Passover (Atzeret shel Pesach), the completion of our atonement, in the sense that through the Spirit, God gives us the power that we need to overcome our tendency toward evil. Yeshua Himself indicated this in John 16:7 (NIV): "*Unless I go away, the Counselor* [Ruach

HaKodesh] *will not come to you; but if I go I will send him to you."*

Shavuot possesses other Messianic significance as well. God spoke of a time when He would write His laws in our hearts (see Jer. 31:32–33). Ezekiel 36:25–27 also mentions His placing the Ruach (Counselor) in our hearts during this same event. So God associates the giving of the Ruach with the placing of His Law in our hearts.

What more appropriate time to visibly place His Ruach in His people than on Shavuot, the feast of the giving of the Law! Notice that Ezekiel connects the giving of the Ruach with the sprinkling of water on us. Moroccan Jews have an ancient custom they perform on Shavuot. They pour water on each other![4] This becomes one more symbol through which Shavuot pictures God as visibly placing the Ruach in the followers of Yeshua.

How to Celebrate Shavuot (Pentecost)

As a congregation, we have started our Shavuot or Pentecost service with a processional. While playing slower music, we have a line of six to eight people walk into the sanctuary single file, each one carrying items such as a menorah, the Bible, sheaves of wheat, banners, the Israeli flag, or two loaves of bread. These items are laid upon the altar. We pray and then begin lively praise and worship. We are celebrating the giving of the Word, the Holy Spirit, and Yeshua— our first fruits!

Another year the Holy Spirit instructed us to set up a *Chupa* (wedding canopy) and place a large bronze pot under it to celebrate a rarely mentioned aspect of Pentecost. The Scripture tells us on Shavuot to give an offering according to how we have been blessed over the last year. This was a powerful act, because the Bible teaches that giving *is* worship. That Pentecost we received the largest offering God has ever given us!

Celebrate this wondrous and supernatural feast day in the Holy Spirit since this is when Father gave us the Ruach. Pray, fast, and ask the Holy Spirit for guidance. Have a Spirit-filled service; advertise in your local newspaper, on television, and on radio. Celebrate the two loaves of bread, Jew and Gentile, by hosting a One New Man celebration. Invite Jews and Gentiles to your Shavuot festival. Worship the God of Israel with lively music and dance, and be free in the Spirit. Worship and dance are powerful ways to involve all people, because these two acts tear down inhibitions in drawing close to God. We have so much to be thankful for and joyous about. God loves us so much that He gave us His Son—and the Holy Spirit. This alone is reason enough for me to want to dance and celebrate.

The world is full of dead congregations and synagogues. We must invite His presence and be filled with

His Spirit. There is nothing more powerful to an unbeliever than experiencing God's power and presence. If you are not filled with the Holy Spirit, ask the Father in Yeshua's name for an infilling of the Holy Spirit. Ask Him to enable you to pray in tongues and speak the Word of God. That is the theme of this holiday—the Word and the Holy Spirit. Peter submitted himself to the Holy Spirit over 2,000 years ago (see Acts 2), and 3,000 Jews were saved. Be filled with the Holy Spirit, speak God's Word, and have 3,000 people saved at your celebration. Walk in the anointing of the One New Man.

Overview of Rosh Hashanah

This biblical holiday originated as *"a sacred assembly, commemorated with trumpet blasts"* (see Lev. 23:23-25 NIV), a holy gathering. Today, we observe it as the New Year because, according to tradition, God created the world on this day. Rosh Hashanah is frequently called the day of remembrance (*Yom HaZikaron*) or the day of judgment (*Yom HaDin*) in view of its inauguration of the days of awe. The first name stresses God's faithfulness to His covenant and promises, the second His righteousness and justice. Still, the holiday conveys joy and delight, as illustrated by the custom of eating sweet things, such as apples dipped in honey.

A very interesting ceremony, *Tashlich*, grew up as part of the Rosh Hashanah observance. Devout Jews go to the edge of a body of water and empty their pockets or throw stones into the water. As they do this, they repeat Micah 7:18-20, which says, *"You will...hurl all our iniquities into the depths of the sea"* (NIV).

Since Rosh Hashanah originated as the memorial of blowing of trumpets, the *shofar* (trumpet) plays an important role. Among other things it symbolizes, according to the rabbis, God's kingship and the coming of the Messianic Age (*Olam Haba*).

Rosh Hashanah has deep Messianic significance. The rabbis taught that one day the shofar would sound and the Messiah would come. When He came, the dead would rise.[5] About a decade after Yeshua, the apostle Paul talked about Messiah's return when he referred to the fact that Yeshua would return for His followers and would thereafter rule the earth as Messiah the King. People refer to this event as the Rapture or Yeshua's Second Coming. In describing the Rapture, Paul said, *"For the Lord Himself will come down from Heaven, with a loud command, with the voice of the archangel and with the trumpet* [shofar] *call of God, and the dead in Christ will rise first"* (1 Thess. 4:16 NIV). This day will certainly be characterized by joy, delight, and sweetness. (That is why we dip apples in honey at this time.)

This particular resurrection is for those who have had, as the Tashlich ceremony reminds us, their sins thrown into the sea by God because they have accepted Yeshua as Messiah. At this time, we will undergo a new creation; we will receive new bodies (see 1 Cor. 15:50-53). Remember, Rosh Hashanah traditionally commemorates the original creation. The Rapture, while being a sign of God's faithfulness to us (*Yom HaZikaron*, day of remembrance), ushers in a time of judgment on the world (*Yom HaDin*, day of judgment).

In Leviticus, the term *memorial* does not mean remembering something that is past. It calls attention to something about to occur. As we observe Rosh Hashanah, we should anticipate the time of Yeshua's return.

Overview of Yom Kippur

Leviticus 23:26-32 describes the Day of Atonement as a most solemn time of introspection and repentance. Those who did not observe this holy day were severely punished. On Yom Kippur only the high priest could enter the most sacred part of the sanctuary. After making a sacrifice for himself, he then brought the blood from the sacrifice that he made for the people (see Lev. 16). On this day, atonement was made for the *whole* nation, as a goat died in place of the people. (According to the most recent studies, *atonement* [in Hebrew, *kippur*] means "ransom by means of a substitute.")

Traditional observance has maintained the solemnity of this great day of repentance. Reminiscences of the Yom Kippur sacrifice still exist among some religious Jews in the custom of *Kapporot*. A chicken is swung over the head as the following is recited: "This is my substitute, this is my commutation; this chicken goes to death; but may I be gathered and enter into a long and happy life and into peace."

Messianic significance abounds. The services during the period of Rosh Hashanah and Yom Kippur refer repeatedly to the binding or sacrifice of Isaac (*Akedah*). The rabbis teach that in some way God accepts the sacrifice of Isaac on our behalf. Isaac beautifully foreshadows the sacrifice of Messiah (see Heb. 11:17-19), whose sacrifice God accepted on our behalf. The *Haftorah* portion on Yom Kippur is the Book of Jonah, the prophet who spent three days in the belly of a large fish before emerging. When Yeshua was challenged to provide evidence for His Messiahship, He pointed to the example of Jonah (see Matt. 12:39-40). He used Jonah as a picture of His own death and resurrection. A *musaf* prayer found in many older Yom Kippur prayer books exhibits additional Messianic significance:

> *The Messiah our righteousness has turned from us. We are alarmed; we have no one to justify us. Our sins and the yoke of our transgressions He bore. He was bruised for our iniquities. He carried on His*

> *shoulders our sins. With His stripes we are healed.*
> *Almighty God, hasten the day that He might come to*
> *us anew; that we may hear from Mt. Lebanon a sec-*
> *ond time through the Messiah ("Oz M'lifnai*
> *B'reshit").*

The apostle Paul writes of a time in the future when all Israel will be redeemed and will have atonement (see Rom. 11:26). The prophet Zechariah also predicted this time of national redemption (see Zech. 12:10; 13:9). In the past, atonement was made for *all* Israel on Yom Kippur. Presently, this holy day looks forward to the time when *all* Israel will accept the atonement provided by the Messiah.

As we await this day, we can celebrate Yom Kippur by thanking God for the atonement available through Yeshua and by praying that more Jewish people will recognize and accept Him as their atonement. The tenor of the day also provides us with an opportunity for self-searching, repentance, and recommitment to God (see 2 Cor. 13:5; 1 John 1:9).

How to Celebrate Rosh Hashanah (New Year) and Yom Kippur (Day of Atonement)

We celebrate Rosh Hashanah and Yom Kippur as one holiday. We start by celebrating Rosh Hashanah with joy and anticipation of the coming of Messiah. We blow the shofar to start the service as Leviticus 23 commands us to do. We then worship the living God in celebratory song and dance. We sound the shofar repetitively as we pray over the congregation and individuals, breaking curses, diseases, and any other afflictions in the name of Yeshua. The shofar blast is like all the prophets of old proclaiming the promises of God. When the shofar is blown, we expect deliverances, healings, salvations, and miracles.

Yeshua shared in Matthew 24 that He would return with a great heavenly sounding of the shofar. Is this the memorial Leviticus 23 is talking about? Are we practicing, every Rosh Hashanah, the much anticipated great heavenly sounding of the shofar announcing the arrival of Yeshua's return? Yeshua shared in Matthew that when He returns, He will judge the nations. Will Yeshua's judgment period take place during the "Ten Days of Awe" that fall between Rosh Hashanah and Yom Kippur?

Will the Yom Kippur that follows Yeshua's judgment period be the "Final Judgment," when our names are kept in or blotted out of the "Lamb's Book of Life?" Yeshua said that *no man knows the day or hour of My return, only the Father knows*" (Matt. 24:36). When we celebrate Rosh Hashanah and Yom Kippur, we do it with a special feeling and sense of anticipated excitement, wondering: "When we blow the shofar this year, will we hear a great sounding from the heavens? Will Yeshua return this year?"

Between Rosh Hashanah and Yom Kippur, the Spirit has directed us to fast together in unity as a congregation. (The Torah calls only for fasting on the day of Yom Kippur.) We search ourselves for anything that is not of the Father and ask Him to remove it from us. We pray for unity among us as a Body and ask God to make us the One New Man. We pray as a corporate Body for the salvation of Israel and the nations. This is also a perfect time to hold evangelistic meetings.

Then we celebrate Yom Kippur, which is traditionally one of the most somber feast days of the year. Yeshua is our High Priest who has gone into the holy of holies once and for all, opening the veil that allows us to have a personal relationship with our Father. We have had Jews visit our service on Yom Kippur and ask why we are so happy on such a somber day. What an opportunity to share Yeshua and bring them into the celebration, explaining that they have a sacrificial covering, that His name is Yeshua, and that we are happy and excited about it. We end our ten-day fast with the sounding of the shofar and teach from Hebrews 9. We celebrate the fact that our sins have been washed away. We then have Communion after worship to enter the holy of holies through the blood of Yeshua and spend time with our Father. That is the miracle of Yom Kippur!

Overview of Sukkot

Leviticus 23:43 portrays Sukkot (Festival of Booths or Tabernacles) as an eight-day period of rejoicing. Although it occurs at harvest time, the festival virtually ignores the harvest theme as it commemorates God's faithfulness to Israel through the wilderness wanderings after they left Egypt.

Traditional observance has maintained the spirit of great rejoicing during Sukkot. As in biblical times, meals are to be eaten in booths as a picture of man's sojourn under God's wings and also as a reminder of freedom from Egypt (see Lev. 23:43). Participants carry the *lulav* branches and the *etrog* (a lemon-like fruit) in a procession through the synagogue and wave the branches in four directions. The waving of the branches goes back to earlier times when Near Eastern people welcomed visiting dignitaries in this way.

The seventh day of the celebration, *Hoshana Rabba*, gets its name from the prayers said on that day. Those prayers begin with the Hebrew *hoshana* ("save now") and include some special Messianic prayers. In tune with the spirit of joy, the participants recite *Hallel* psalms (113–118) during the week's celebration. It all culminates on the ninth day with *Simchat Torah*, the day of rejoicing over God's gift of the Law to the Jewish people.

During the era of the second temple, two events that no longer take place highlighted the celebration. Water drawn from a nearby source was brought to the temple and poured out by the altar as Isaiah 12:3 was repeated: *"With joy you will draw water from the wells of salvation"* (NIV). The torchlight parade, brilliantly illuminating the temple at night, stood out as the other great event, possibly reflecting a verse from one of the Hallel psalms: *"The Lord is God, and He has made His light shine upon us"* (Ps. 118:27 NIV).

Yeshua chose these two events to highlight His mission as Messiah. As the water was being poured by the altar, He announced, *"If anyone is thirsty, let him come to Me and drink. Whoever believes in Me, as the Scripture has said, streams of living water will flow from within him"* (John 7:37-38 NIV). As torches lit up the temple, He shouted, *"I am the light of the world. Whoever follows Me...will have the light of life"* (John 8:12 NIV).

Messianic significance also abounds in the celebration as traditionally observed since temple days. Two verses from one of the Hallel psalms stand out: *"The stone the builders rejected has become the capstone"* (Ps. 118:22 NIV). This beautifully pictures the time when Yeshua will reign as Messiah, the King over the earth. The waving of the lulav, that Near Eastern form of welcome, will be directed toward Him in that day. One of the prayers of Hoshana Rabba echoes this welcome to Messiah:

A voice heralds, heralds and saith: Turn unto Me and be ye saved, today if ye hear My voice. Behold the man who springs forth, Branch[6] is his name....But to His anointed, the Messiah, He giveth grace. Grant salvation to the eternal people. To David and to His seed[7] forever....

This prayer eagerly anticipates the coming of the Messianic Kingdom. Then people will rejoice in the presence of the living Torah, Yeshua, the One called the Word of God (see John 1:1-14). That *Simchat Torah* will have no rivals in its joy and celebration. (*Simchat Torah* means "rejoicing over the law" and occurs immediately following the Feast of Tabernacles.) Zechariah 14:16-19 describes this as a time when all nations, not just Israel, will keep the festival of Sukkot and live in booths.

As we celebrate Sukkot each year, we can anticipate that time when the booths will no longer picture our present sojourn under God's wings. *Then* they will remind us of the past, *before* the reign of *Yeshua HaMashiach* the King. In the meantime, the booths remind us to depend on God and not on material goods (see Matt. 6:25-33).

How to Celebrate Sukkot (Feast of Tabernacles)

Sukkot commemorates the 40-year period during which the children of Israel wandered in the desert, living in temporary shelters. During this festival, we build a *sukkah* (temporary shelter, booth) in our back-yard. You can also put it on your balcony if you live in a multifamily home, such as an apartment. If neither of these are possibilities, you can share a sukkah with friends or family who do have one. Various plans to build a sukkah can be found in your local library or on the Internet. It is common practice, and highly com-mendable, to decorate your sukkah with seasonal dec-orations celebrating the harvest and God's provision. In the United States dried squash, corn, colorful fall foliage, grapes, and pumpkins are used to decorate the sukkah.

When seeing a decorated sukkah for the first time, Americans remark on how much it reminds them of the American holiday of Thanksgiving. The early set-tlers of America who began the Thanksgiving tradition were a deeply religious people. They looked to the Bible for guidance in expressing their gratitude to God for the bountiful harvest and their survival of another year in the new land. They based their early Thanks-giving celebrations in part on the biblical holiday of Sukkot.

Sukkot is our favorite feast day. In our backyard we build a large sukkah, approximately 12 feet by 12 feet, line the walls with bales of hay, outline the framework with strands of white holiday lights, and invite family, neighbors, and friends to worship in our sukkah every evening for the length of the feast.

Sukkot is the feast in which we also celebrate the birth of Yeshua, who is the Son of the living God and who is our Salvation and Provision, our Shelter, and our Provider. It is so peaceful to sit in the sukkah on a beautiful fall evening with friends and family, worshiping God in song and dance, and rejoicing in the birth of our Messiah. This feast day is the most joyful of all.

In past years the Holy Spirit has led us to build a small sukkah in our sanctuary. We decorated it with brightly colored fall leaves, clusters of grapes, pumpkins, squash, and small bales of hay. As we danced and worshiped God, people were healed.

One woman was healed from colon cancer while dancing before the Lord. Another woman had endured several surgeries on her shoulder trying to resolve the constant pain issues. As she worshiped the Lord, the Holy Spirit touched her shoulder, and she immediately removed the sling she had been wearing for five months because she was healed!

One year we built our sukkah and placed a crib under it with baby Yeshua in it as our dance team danced to the song "Mary, Did You Know?" We then sang songs proclaiming our love for God and our remembrance of His gift of Yeshua as our Messiah.

Invite unsaved Jewish and Gentile friends to your services or home sukkah to dance and worship before the God of Israel. God moves mightily on His appointed times, His holy convocations. People will see Yeshua in these celebrations.

The Holidays Outside the Leviticus Cycle

Overview of Purim

Purim commemorates the events of the scroll of Esther, as we relive our deliverance from Haman and take renewed faith in outliving the Hamans of other times. The celebration provides a joyous, carnival-type atmosphere. Haman attempted to exterminate the Jews, so the holiday is a reminder of God's preservation of and commitment to Israel. But in the context of Purim, it reminds us of God's *preservation during our exile.* The disorderly, raucous, carnival nature of Purim then serves to remind us of God's preservation of our people through the years of exile until Messiah rules and disorder disappears.

How to Celebrate Purim

Purim is a great way to teach others about God's plans and purposes for Israel despite anti-Semitism.

We prepare to celebrate Purim as we do the feast days. We begin in prayer, seeking the leading of the Holy Spirit. We have previously hosted a Purim play, acting out the story of Purim, merging the traditional story with modern vernacular, dressing and portraying Haman as a terrorist or modern Middle Eastern dictator. (It is open to interpretation.) We had Queen Vashti act like a rebellious teenager, refusing to submit to authority, and portrayed Mordecai and Esther as godly examples of holiness and obedience, submitting themselves to God's will instead of their own. It is a powerful message to Jew and Gentile alike.

The play provided a wonderful venue to teach children and adults about God's plan for Israel and Jerusalem, and about the prophetic importance of the Jewish people in the last days. It reemphasizes God's desire for us to stand with Israel and the Jewish people, even at the cost of our own lives. Mordecai's words spoken to Queen Esther are valid for all believers today:

> *Don't think for a moment that you will escape there in the palace when all other Jews are killed. If you keep quiet at a time like this, deliverance for the Jews will arise from some other place, but you and your relatives will die. What's more, who can say but that you have been elevated to the palace for just such a time as this?* (Esther 4:13-14 NLT).

We have also celebrated Purim by selecting seven or eight individuals to read an assigned portion from the Book of Esther before the congregation. We pass out noisemakers before the service. Whenever the name Haman is mentioned, the people are instructed to boo and hiss. When the name Mordecai is read, the congregation cheers and uses noisemakers. This has such an impact on the children who remain in the sanctuary for this reading. They listen intently to the story, waiting to hear the name of Mordecai or Haman mentioned. We conclude the reading with joyous praise and worship, including dance. The people of Israel are alive today because of divine intervention. What a tremendous reason to celebrate and worship the living God.

Overview of Hanukkah

Hanukkah reminds us of the victory won by the Maccabees in 165 B.C., which insured the purity of the worship of God and preserved the distinctiveness of Israel and the Jewish identity. After God granted this tremendous victory, the people cleansed and rededicated the temple. The Syrian ruler, Antiochus, had defiled the temple and turned it into a heathen shrine. Therefore, Hanukkah originated as the festival of the dedication or cleansing of the temple.

Yeshua used the Feast of Dedication (see John 10:22) to proclaim Himself as the Good Shepherd (see

John 10:1-18). In the Jewish writings, shepherds frequently represented the leaders of Israel, both good and bad. (The Maccabees, for example, would have been considered among the good shepherds.) Yeshua, therefore, announced Himself as the Good Shepherd *par excellence*.

The Book of Daniel predicted the rise of Antiochus and his defiling of the temple (see Dan. 8; 11). Daniel also used Antiochus to represent a figure in the future whom Christian theologians call the antichrist (antimessiah). He will also defile the temple (in this case, the third temple, which is not yet built). The antimessiah will cause great persecution for the Jewish people, a time known as Jacob's trouble (see Jer. 30:4-7; Zech. 13:8-9). At this time, Yeshua the Messiah, as the great Shepherd-leader, will come and win a tremendous victory greater than that won by Yehudah the Maccabee (see Zech. 12-14; 1 Pet. 5:4). He will save Israel and establish His worldwide rule.

Hanukkah looks back to a victory and the preservation of the Jewish people when they were *in the land*. For us, it looks forward to a time when our Jewish people will be preserved despite intense suffering. This preservation, again while the Jewish people are in the land, will culminate in the victory won by the Great Shepherd Yeshua.

Thus, Purim pictures our preservation from our enemies while we were in exile, and Hanukkah pictures our preservation while we were in the land. Both anticipate the reign of Messiah.

How to Celebrate Hanukkah

Hanukkah is a story of miracles, sanctification, and salvation. What a fantastic time of year to share Yeshua. It is no accident that the Savior of the world was miraculously conceived during the Festival of Lights. We celebrated this miraculous holiday one year in worship and dance. Our dance team did the Hanukkah service, telling the story of Hanukkah and Yeshua through seven worship dance songs. Between the dances, a narrator shared stories of Hanukkah miracles from various periods of history such as the Holocaust, Russian pogroms, and the Maccabee period. We have had numerous visitors receive Yeshua at this holiday service as well. We advertised our Hanukkah service in our local newspaper and on the radio, bringing in Jew and Gentile, saved and unsaved alike. So many people are curious that they come by the hundreds to see what this holiday festival is all about.

One year a congregant wrote and directed a Hanukkah play, sharing the miraculous Hanukkah story and the correlation between the Festival of Lights and the Light of the World, Yeshua. This play touched many lives as people came to the altar to rededicate and cleanse their temples (their hearts) before God. And some received Yeshua. Again, these celebrations teach the children and provide an opportunity for the Body to come together, worship, and remember all the miraculous things God has done for us.

Final Thoughts From Rabbi Eric Carlson

Yeshua fulfilled the feast days so we can be free to enter the Father's presence, fellowship with Him, be filled with the Holy Spirit, and know God's will. God gave us the feast days to practice for the celebrations we will enjoy when we enter Heaven. The feasts are a way to share Yeshua with both Jews and Gentiles. They are a prophetic vision of what is to come. When Yeshua returns, all nations will come to Jerusalem to celebrate the feast days. The feasts are our biblical culture that bind us together with Israel through shalom and unity in Yeshua. The feast days are God's and, in His words, are to be celebrated forever. Celebrate the feasts, filled with the Holy Spirit, as the One New Man—Yeshua!

After every feast day or holiday celebration, we *oneg*, or have "holiday delight." How do we oneg? We prepare traditional holiday or feast-day food items (mostly as a potluck dinner; families will bring in their favorite holiday recipe). We decorate a fellowship hall according to the current holiday theme. On Hanukkah we use a lot of candles. For Sukkot we use fall foliage, pumpkins, and gourds. We then invite everyone who attended the service to this hall to oneg with us—to fellowship with one another and eat. We have had numerous people attend our celebration services, then come and oneg with us, asking questions one-on-one in the fellowship hall (which is a very unimposing room), and then receive Yeshua. Oneg provides a comfortable, family atmosphere where people feel very relaxed and are open to discussing and asking questions about Yeshua. Oneg helps us reclaim the fellowship and intimacy of personal interaction that has been lost in an impersonal, electronic society.

10

THE LAW OF EVANGELISM

ONE RAINY DAY in Rockville, Maryland, I decided to visit the Judaic library at the Jewish Community Center. A book on the Jews of China caught my eye. It showed pictures of Chinese Jews from Kaifeng whose ancestors had come to China many generations earlier. They came as silk merchants and lived in cities along the "Silk Route." I also noted the reference to Isaiah 49:12, *"Surely these shall come from afar; look! Those from the north and the west, and these from the land of Sinim."* The author said the word *Sinim* is Hebrew for "China." Imagine, I thought, God predicted there would be Jews in China. I had never even heard of a Chinese Jew. Further, God said they would return to Israel in the last days.

In 1995, Bob Weiner, a visiting speaker, told the local church I attended that revival had started in China. Pastor Bill Ligon asked if I wanted to team-up with him to take a tour group there. I immediately said, "Yes, if we can go to Kaifeng." My motivation in going to Kaifeng was the Law of Evangelism. I knew if we reached out to the Jew, God would bless our efforts to reach all people.

In Kaifeng, I met a Chinese Jew who took me to his family cemetery. He proudly showed me 12 generations of his Jewish ancestors. Another Chinese Jew told me, "I am a Jew. I told my son he is a Jew, and he must live in Israel!" This man knew nothing about Judaism or Christianity. How could he know that thousands of years earlier God had recorded in the Bible that Jews from China would return to Israel? Since that time, he and his entire family have immigrated to Israel. This family and many other Chinese Jews have received Yeshua as Messiah!

As part of the tour, we brought singers and dancers to Kaifeng to conduct a Feast of Tabernacles celebration. This event was televised throughout the entire city. When we went to the Jew first, God opened up a door to reach the whole area.

Don't Compromise

A best-selling Christian author has written a book saying that it is unbiblical to "go to the Jew first" with the gospel. He argues that Jewish people have suffered so much they should not be targeted for evangelism by overzealous Christians. A well-meaning Christian who reads this will feel no need to evangelize the Jew. Many believers who say they love the Jewish people and Israel share this anti-Semitic thinking. I'm sure they genuinely love the Jew and Israel, but they need to realize that the most anti-Semitic act is to *not* share the gospel with them. They must be careful not to value their relationship with the Jewish community more highly than their obedience to God's Word.

It is true that, after all these centuries of persecution by so-called Christians, we must love the Jew. Only acts of supernatural love will melt the centuries of misunderstandings. But don't fall into the trap of a love without Yeshua.

Several years ago, a pastor friend of mine shared a very poignant story. He had befriended an Orthodox rabbi. Over the years, this rabbi taught this Baptist pastor many Jewish understandings from the Jewish Scriptures. Then they lost touch. After many years, the pastor called the rabbi. The rabbi was in an old-age home and burst into tears when he heard the voice of his friend. The rabbi really loved the Baptist pastor. Shortly thereafter, the rabbi died. After my friend told me this story, I looked him in the eye and asked, "Did you ever share the gospel with him?" He paused and I could see what was going through his mind. Although he didn't say this, I knew it had never dawned on him to share Yeshua with his Jewish friend. Unfortunately, this is a typical example of the poison that has infected many Gentile Christians. May the words of Ezekiel 3:17–18 and Acts 4:12 ring in our ears:

> *Son of man, I have made you a watchman for the house of Israel.... When I say to the wicked, "You shall surely die," and you give him no warning...his blood I will require at your hand* (Ezekiel 3:17-18).
>
> *Nor is there salvation in any other, for there is no other name under heaven given among men by which we must be saved* (Acts 4:12).

Follow the Pattern

The Law of Evangelism is found in Romans 1:16: *"For I am not ashamed of the gospel of* [Messiah], *for it is the power of God to salvation for everyone who believes, for* **the Jew first** *and also for the Greek."* This was God's *historical* order to reach the world, but it is also God's *spiritual* order.

This pattern is found throughout Scripture. When God wanted to redeem the world, He started with Abram, who became Abraham, the father of the Jewish people. God went to the Jew first to reach the world. When Yeshua went to the Jew first, it opened up a supernatural door of evangelism for all people. Yeshua commanded His disciples, *"Go rather to the lost sheep of the house of Israel"* (Matt. 10:6). The Messiah knew that planting a seed to the Jew first would open the door to evangelize the world. Since the Jewish people have been spread to the four corners of the earth (see Isa. 11:12), when you go to the Jews, you reach virtually everyone else too. Paul also followed this pattern in Romans 1:16.

The principle that causes the Law of Evangelism to operate is found in Genesis 12:3. God promises to bless those who bless the Jewish people. As we sow seed into the Jewish people by sharing the good news with them, we will reap an abundant harvest among the Gentiles. John Owen, one of the greatest Puritan theologians, knew this amazing truth about going to the Jew first. He said, "There is not any promise anywhere of raising up a kingdom unto the Lord Jesus Christ in this world but it is either expressed, or clearly intimated, that the beginning of it must be with the Jews."[1]

God says He will pour out His Spirit on all flesh in the last days. As a result, Jewish sons and daughters will prophesy (see Joel 2:28). The Jewish people will experience a major revival. The prophet Joel says this will happen at the time when the nations try to divide up the land of Israel (see Joel 3:2). And it will be the catalyst for the greatest revival in history. Zechariah says:

Thus says the Lord of hosts: "*In those days ten men from every language of the nations shall grasp the sleeve* [fringes of the prayer shawl] *of a Jewish man, saying, 'Let us go with you, for we have heard that God is with you'*" (Zechariah 8:23).

God will cause His former rain (the Spirit of God on the Jewish people) and His latter rain (the Spirit of God on Christians) to come down at *the same time* (see Joel 2:23). Rain brings life for the harvest. This specific miracle has never happened in history. The supernatural downpour of the two rains simultaneously will bring forth a harvest that will result in multitudes being saved!

You and Your House

When I tell believers they need to reach the Jewish people with the gospel, some are exasperated. "But Sid," they protest, "I have tried to share Yeshua with Jewish people. They are just not interested."

This is God's appointed time to reach Israel. But it can't be done by man's methods. I'm an expert on how it *cannot* be done. I have tried just about everything. Although most of these methods have worked to some degree, the revival prophesied in Joel 2:28 has not fully manifested. If it is God's time to reach the Jewish people with the gospel and to form the One New Man

Glorious Congregation, then how will it take place?

God has given me a prophetic example through my father. When I accepted the Lord, he was shocked, outraged, and embarrassed. My dad was born in Poland into a traditional Jewish family. To say the least, he was not raised to love Christianity. He told me that when he was a young boy his father would spit at a church as they walked past. Whenever I talked about Yeshua, the conversation ended in shouting, anger, and much hurt. My public, vocal witness for Yeshua brought him shame.

My mother was another story. She was also Jewish, but she was born in America. Although she attended the traditional synagogue to please my father, she was not as fervent. When I accepted the Lord, she wasn't happy, but she never let it interfere with her love for me. She was grateful that my experience with God had restored my marriage and made me a far more responsible person. While my mom tolerated my beliefs, she was not quick to follow them. When I shared prophecies that proved Yeshua was the Jewish Messiah, it didn't faze her. When I prayed for her and others and they were healed, it interested her but didn't change her. Finally, as she observed the peace and fulfillment I had over many years, the Lord broke through, and she received Him as the Jewish Messiah.

Immediately after I had my experience with Yeshua, I began to share my testimony. Wherever I spoke I asked people to pray for my father's salvation. My mother was not so hopeful. She would sigh and tell me, "Your father will never believe in Jesus!"

I replied without the slightest doubt, "I *know* he will become a believer." From that point on I began to say often, "I *know* my father will become a believer." I said it so many times that I began to believe it. My mother didn't want me to be disappointed. She was sure it was impossible for a Jewish person like my father to believe. But Yeshua says in Mark 9:23, *"If you can believe, **all** things are possible...."* And I had long since moved from hope to faith.

After Mom died, my father asked me to go to the synagogue daily for a year and say a memorial prayer (*Kaddish*) for her. I knew it would not do her any good because she was already in Heaven. But, for my father's sake, I went and said a prayer. Many people at the synagogue, who did not like that I was an outspoken believer, still told my father that I was a good son for going every day to the synagogue. After that year, my dad had many close calls with death. I remember telling people: "Dad can't die. He hasn't received Yeshua yet."

But then I got the call from my sister, Shirley. My father was dying. Shirley and her husband, Marc, had been believers in the Messiah almost as long as I had. "It looks bad," Shirley told me. "You'd better come." Without hesitation, I booked a flight.

Something unusual had happened to me a week earlier. A tangible, wonderful peace from God had come all over my body. This had happened before, but it was different this time. It stayed with me 24 hours a day, and it kept getting stronger. I didn't know the reason for it, but I was grateful.

When I arrived, I met my sister at the hospital, and we went straight to the intensive care unit. My dad was 83 and had prostate cancer. Since the cancer had invaded his bones, we knew he could die at any moment. His voice was so weak he could barely speak above a whisper. I asked, "Dad, don't you want to be in the same place as Mom? She used to say, 'Heaven must be such a wonderful place.' Do you want to make Yeshua your Messiah and Lord?"

He replied, "Yes," and we prayed.

Then my sister said, "Sid, I didn't hear him."

I responded, "Shirley, that was *good* for Dad. *I* heard him."

She put her hands on her hips and said, "I'm not sure. Dad, do you want to make Yeshua your Messiah and Lord?"

My father got his old spunk back and belted out, "Yes!"

With that, Shirley began to jump up and down and scream very loudly, "Thank You, Yeshua! Thank You!"

My sister was a conservative schoolteacher, so this outburst was totally out of character for her. Besides, in the intensive care unit everyone is *supposed* to remain very quiet. I tried to calm her down—to no avail. She said, "I promised the Lord I would jump for joy when Dad was saved!"

My father went to Heaven the next day.

The Anointing Destroys the Yoke

Many have witnessed to Jewish people without any visible signs of success. As a result, they have stopped witnessing. But now we are in a new season. This is the set time to favor Zion. God must restore the Jewish branches to the olive tree. We cannot have the "glorious church" until the middle wall of separation comes down between Jew and Gentile to birth the One New Man. God is once again having mercy on Israel.

How was my father saved? Remember the anointing that came upon me a week before he died? *"And the yoke will be destroyed because of the anointing..."* (Isa. 10:27). The anointing of the Holy Spirit destroys the demonic yokes of unbelief. Get ready for the anointing for Jewish evangelism that is being poured out. All things are possible to those who believe. If a Jew like my father can be saved, so can the Jewish people God will have cross your path! It is *"not by might nor by power, but by My Spirit, says the Lord of hosts"* (Zech. 4:6).

A Lamb for a House

I am blessed because my entire family knows Yeshua. This is God's norm. In the Book of Exodus, God says the lamb sacrificed at Passover is for the *entire* household (see Exod. 12:3). Noah's entire household was saved from the Flood (see Genesis 7:1). The scarlet cord, which represents the blood, protected Rahab's entire family from being killed (see Josh. 2:18). Joshua knew the heart of God for families to be saved when he said, *"But as for me and **my house,** we will serve the Lord"* (Josh. 24:15). When Cornelius, a Gentile, came to accept Yeshua as Savior, it resulted in his whole family being saved as well (see Acts 10:24,44). In Acts 16:31, Paul said to the Philippian jailer, *"Believe on the Lord* [Yeshua the Messiah], *and you will be saved, **you and your household."***

The Jewish law for family evangelism applies not just to one member of a household but the entire *mishpochah* (family). You *and* your house will be saved! A Lamb for a house!

11

GETTING BACK TO BASICS

MY CHILDHOOD MEMORIES of Passover include the empty place setting at the table for Elijah. Every year we expected the prophet to announce the coming of the Messiah. I would even go to the door and open it just in case Elijah was waiting outside. And every year I would be disappointed. This practice comes from Malachi 4:5-6:

> *Behold, I will send you Elijah the prophet before the coming of the great and dreadful day of the Lord. And he will turn the hearts of the fathers to the children, and the hearts of the children to their fathers, lest I come and strike the earth with a curse.*

As I grew up, I realized that many traditional Jews did not believe Elijah would ever come—it was just a fable. After I became a Messianic Jew, I learned that Elijah had already come. Yeshua made it clear that

Elijah in Malachi's prophecy referred to John the Baptist (see Matt. 17:10-13). Luke 1:17 says that John would walk *"in the spirit and power of Elijah."* In other words, the same spirit that was on Elijah would be on John.

But what about the rest of the prophecy? Paul tells us that the fathers of the faith are Jewish. (See Romans 9:4-5.) The children represent Christians because they have received a spiritual heritage from the Jewish fathers—Abraham, Isaac, and Jacob. So Malachi warns us that if Jews and Christians are not unified in the last days, we will receive a curse instead of a blessing.

Remember, the favor of God followed the Jewish tabernacle (see Gen. 12:3). Wherever the tabernacle went, it brought blessing to those who were obedient to God. When the Jewish people are restored to the olive tree, it will bring the blessing of God. This is exactly what Paul saw in Romans:

> *Now if their* [the Jewish people's] *fall is riches for the world, and their failure riches for the Gentiles, how much more their fullness!* ...*For if their being cast away is the reconciling of the world, what will their acceptance be but life from the dead?* (Rom. 11:12,15).

Get ready for the new outpouring of God's Spirit on the dry, dead bones of Israel. It will bring blessings and resurrection life back to the Church. It will release the greatest revival in history.

The devil will not take this lying down. Watch out for the greatest deception in Church history. Replacement Theology will be rampant. Another of the devil's strategies to delay this next move of God will be to make the Jewish roots movement legalistic. Religious spirits will cause some Christians to believe that if they don't say God's name in Hebrew or if they don't worship on Saturday, it will cost them their salvation. They will try to make those who celebrate traditional Christian holidays feel like second-class citizens.

Don't get me wrong. I believe there are supernatural blessings in New Covenant expressions of celebrating the feasts. I love to refer to Jesus by His Hebrew name, Yeshua. I love to have my Shabbat (Sabbath) on Saturday—the biblical day God selected. I know that centuries ago many Church traditions were merged with pagan practices for political and anti-Jewish reasons. I know how, after this happened, the Church moved from intimacy and power to dead religion. But *please* do not commit the same error by legislating something God Himself is restoring in New Testament freedom. Let us provoke others to jealousy by the outpouring of God's Spirit and love and power when we worship Him on biblical feast days.

On the other hand, the same religious spirits are at work in the Gentile Church. Some Christians make you feel as if Sunday worship is required for salvation. Others act as if you are betraying the faith if you object to the paganism mixed into Easter and Christmas or if you use Hebrew names. For revival to spread we will need a lot more loving and a lot less judging.

We are approaching the time of Jacob's trouble. *"Alas! For that day is great, so that none is like it; and it is the time of Jacob's trouble, but he shall be saved out of it"* (Jer. 30:7). This will be the worst time of persecution in history, first for the Jew and then for the Christian. When persecution hits, which day we worship or how we worship will not be as important as *Who* we worship.

The supernatural blessings that will be released when the Church evangelizes the Jew are needed now! The salvation of Israel is necessary for the emergence of the Elijah generation, and the Elijah generation will prepare the way of the Lord. The Gentile Christian needs the piece of the puzzle that the Jewish believer has, and the Jewish believer needs the part of the puzzle that the Gentile Christian has—and we all need Yeshua. These are the days of Elijah!

The One New Man Glorious Congregation

What would the church be like today if we started from scratch and just followed the Scriptures? What would happen if we removed all tradition from Judaism and Christianity, and Jews and Christians came together as one? Let me introduce you to the Glorious

Congregation—the emergence of the One New Man—Yeshua!

Although Malachi is the last book in the Christian Old Testament, Second Chronicles is the last book in the Jewish Old Testament, or as we Jewish people would say, the Tenach. The Tenach presents the books of Scripture in a different order. I believe that the last words in the Tenach must have great prophetic significance. The Tenach closes with this prophetic word:

> *Thus hath said Cyrus the king of Persia, "All the kingdoms of the earth hath the Lord the God of Heaven given me; and he* **hath charged me to build him a house in Jerusalem, which is in Judah.** *Whoever there is among you of all his people, may the Lord his God be with him, and let him go up"* (2 Chron. 36:23).

The spiritual fulfillment of these words will reach its highest expression in the One New Man Congregation of Jewish and Gentile believers.

God says we must build Him a house (temple). (See Ephesians 2:14–15;22.) His objective is to *"gather together in one all things in* [Messiah]*"* (Eph. 1:10). When the wall between Jew and Gentile is removed, the spiritual temple, God's dwelling place, will be restored, and this One New Man will release resurrection power to the Church that Paul calls *"life from the dead"* (Rom. 11:15).

How can the devil stop the explosion of God's power? *How can he stop the building of the temple?* If the foundation is destroyed, the temple cannot be built. What is the strategy? Stop Jews from seeing the Messiah and becoming one with Gentile believers.

The Tabernacle of David

The tabernacle of David in First Chronicles 16 is a prophetic symbol of the One New Man. In the tabernacle of David, no separation existed between the people and God. It had no holy of holies where the High Priest could only enter once a year. Everyone experienced God's presence 24/7. David instituted daily praise before the Lord and the Levites worshiped God with the songs of David (see 1 Chron. 16:37).

The tabernacle of David prophesied by Amos is also a type of the One New Man Glorious Congregation.

"On that day I will raise up the tabernacle [house or family] *of David* [the Jewish people], *which has fallen down, and repair its damages; I will raise up its ruins, and rebuild it as in the days of old; that they may possess the remnant of Edom* [Septuagint reads "mankind"], *and all the Gentiles who are called by My name," says the Lord who does this thing* (Amos 9:11-12).

In this passage, God promised that when revival hits the tabernacle of David (the Jewish people) it will cause a revival among the Gentiles. In fact, this was the proof text that convinced the apostles at the Jerusalem Council meeting that they should evangelize the Gentiles (see Acts 15:16-17). Amos 9:13 says that the blessings of revival will be so great that the reaper will not be able to gather all the harvest before the next planting season begins. The plowman will overtake the reaper.

If Gentiles were the missing part of the Church at the time of the Jerusalem Council meeting of Acts 15, who is missing now? After Yeshua died, the veil of the temple was torn in two (see Matt. 27:51). Now nothing should separate us from intimacy with God. Yet the middle wall of division (veil) between Jews and Gentiles hinders the Church from achieving its full destiny in God (see Eph. 2:14). If we want to see and experience God's glory here on earth, then we need to knock down the wall of division that separates us.

Do You Want to See His Face?

Moses saw God's glory, but he could not look at His face. *"And* [Moses] *said, 'Please, show me Your glory.'... But He said, 'You cannot see My face; for no man shall see Me, and live'"* (Exod. 33:18, 20). After being in God's presence, the glory on Moses' face was so intense that he had to wear a veil or the brightness would blind the people who looked at him, as though they were gazing directly into the sun.

The glory of the Old Covenant tabernacle was so thick that, at times, Moses could not even enter (see Exod. 40:35). When the cloud of God's glory filled Solomon's temple, the priests could not stand (see 2 Chron. 5:14). Under the New Covenant, our bodies are temples of the Holy Spirit (see 1 Cor. 6:19). If the Old Covenant glory was so strong, how much greater will the glory be that will fill our New Covenant temples when Jew and Gentile become One New Man in Yeshua?

When will this happen? Psalm 102:13-16 states:

> *You will arise and have mercy on Zion; for the time to favor her, yes, the set time, has come. For Your servants take pleasure in her stones, and show favor to her dust. So the nations shall fear the name of the Lord, and all the kings of the earth Your glory. For the Lord shall build up Zion; He shall appear in His glory.*

When the servants, the Jewish people, take pleasure in (or return to) Israel, the Lord will build up Zion (Jerusalem). When the Lord builds up Zion, He will appear in His glory. This prophecy was written for *"the generation to come"* (Ps. 102:18). The Hebrew could be translated, "for the *last* generation."

This last generation will be uniquely created to restore Davidic praise and worship in order to prepare a tabernacle for the King. Romans 9:4 says the Jewish people will bring the "service" or "worship." This will create a new dimension of worship. As magnificent Levitical worship is restored, it will bring an outpouring of the same glory that was in Solomon's temple. The Old Covenant glory is the former rain. When the former rain teams up with the latter rain, or the New Covenant glory, we will experience a move of God like the world has never seen.

Miracles in Kiev

The closest thing to this outpouring that I have experienced is in the world's largest Messianic Jewish congregation in Kiev, Ukraine. The leader, Rabbi Boris, is always in the Spirit, where he receives direction from God. When he implements these instructions, the congregation flourishes. What is his secret? Boris has surrendered to the Holy Spirit.

Over 1,000 Jews and Gentiles gather to worship every Saturday in Boris' congregation. Normally there are at least 100 instant healings in *every* service. God instructed Boris to use old-style Chassidic (Orthodox Jewish) worship. The music and dancing are so infectious that almost everyone joins in.

Music usually precedes the move of God. The music that will usher in the One New Man will be a brand-new song. It will be the same music described in Revelation 15:3—the song of Moses (Jew) and the song of the Lamb (Christian) becoming one. It will be a love song from the Bride to her heavenly Bridegroom, from the Church to Yeshua. Eye has not seen and ear has not heard what will happen as the Bride and Bridegroom increase in intimacy.

Have you ever been to a Jewish wedding? As great as they are on earth, I want to invite you to the best one ever. You have a golden invitation to the marriage supper of the Lamb.

Full Circle

Everything is about to come full circle. The first people to get the good news were the Jews, but they will also be the last to get the gospel. Yeshua said, "*So the last will be first, and the first last...*" (Matt. 20:16). God is about ready to move the Jewish people and the nation of Israel to center stage once again. It is as though we are watching a video of Church history in reverse. The closer we get to the return of the Messiah, the more we will look like the first Church, and the more the world will focus on the Jew and Israel.

The restoration of the Jewish roots of the Church is happening before our eyes. The Church will become more Hebraic in culture. Jewish believers will move into leadership in the Church, just as it was at first. There also will be a restoration of the temple, both physically and spiritually. And, of course, the Jews are already returning to Israel.

Although I have presented many of the ingredients of the One New Man Congregation, it will include much more. The one thing for sure is that the next, greatest, and last move of God's Spirit will be different from anything any of us has ever seen.

12

TRADITION

DID YOU EVER PLAY the game "telephone" as a child? One person whispers a phrase into another person's ear. By the time the message passes through several people, it is completely distorted. This is what has happened in the Church. Down through the ages, customs and traditions have distorted the truth of God's Word. We have wandered from the old paths. We need a more far-reaching reformation than the one started by Martin Luther. We need to return to the God of our fathers. All the way back.

Many years ago I heard about a unique tradition at an Orthodox synagogue in Washington, DC. Whenever someone went to the platform to read from the Torah, he would bend his knees and lower his head about a foot, then stand back up before he got to the Torah scroll. One day a curious member asked, "Rabbi, why do we dip so low before reading the Torah?" The rabbi explained that the synagogue had previously been located in the basement of another building. Just in front of the Torah was a low water pipe. The only way to get to the Scriptures without hitting your head was to dip low.

As a Jew, I have experienced enough tradition to last a lifetime. But Christianity is loaded with tradition as well. Tradition is a human problem. We all have patterns with which we feel most comfortable. A pastor feels he has to accommodate all these comfort zones. If he is unsuccessful, he often burns out or quits. If he succeeds, the spiritual development of the church is hindered.

Religious groups that have been around the longest have the most tradition. For instance, we Jewish people have more tradition than the Catholics. The Catholics have more tradition than the Protestants. Pentecostals have more tradition than the Charismatics who, in turn, have more tradition than the Word of Faith movement. You get the idea. After going to a specific church for many years, tradition sets in. You find yourself uncomfortable in other expressions in the Body of Messiah.

What would happen if the church that always wears choir robes suddenly cast them aside? What if the drums, bass, and guitar were to get very loud in a traditional service? What would happen if the pastor appeared on a Sunday morning with no tie or suit? On the other hand, for those of you who attend a church where the members dress casually, how would you react if your pastor showed up in a suit and tie?

What if there was no "special" music before the pastor spoke? Or what if the pastor suddenly started shaking under the power of God and others began wailing and travailing in the Spirit? What if a mighty wind with flames of fire came into your church building and people started speaking in tongues and acting like they were drunk? (See Acts 2:1-15.) What would happen if our congregations were more "God-sensitive" than "seeker-sensitive"? What is more important: God showing up or your traditional order of service?

If the pastor yields to the Spirit, he will immediately start a membership drive—he will drive the members who are preventing revival right out of his church. Some members will say, "I have been a believer for thirty years, and God has never worked that way." Others will be uncomfortable because the pastor is preaching the lordship of Yeshua—not a watered-down version of a cheap life insurance policy. It will not be two hymns, a hum, and out by noon. The entertainment mode will be gone forever (may it rest in peace). On occasion the pastor might be so caught up in worship that a service could end without him bringing something from the Word. Instead, members will experience the Living Word. Children and teenagers will not be shipped out to watch videos. They will all be at the front of the church weeping for the lost.

Home Sweet Home (Church)

The early Church met in houses. Acts 2:46 says that they were *"breaking bread from house to house."* Every believer participated at these house meetings. Paul wrote, *"Whenever you come together,* **each of you** *has a psalm, has a teaching, has a tongue, has a revelation, has an interpretation..."* (1 Cor. 14:26). How is this possible in a large meeting? It's not. An ideal place to do this is in home meetings, like the early Church did.

The emphasis in these meetings will not be on the "one man show," but on the "One New Man Body." The people will really get to know one another. They will become *mishpochah* (Hebrew for "family") by sharing meals, sharing their lives, and demonstrating God's Kingdom on earth by caring for one another. The leader's job will be to offer maturity by leading lightly while surrendering control of the meetings to the lordship of the Holy Spirit.

Instead of a worship team leading the music, anyone in the group can lead. The Holy Spirit may bring a song to someone's mind that relates to whatever is being discussed or prayed that stirs the person to worship. As that person begins to sing, the others will catch the moment and follow in Spirit-prompted song.

The same is true for prayer. Conversations with the Lord are interspersed between other elements of worship, as if He was there with them. In fact, He is!

Sometimes a declaration of praise or thanksgiving will begin with one person responding to what was in his heart and will go around the group. Under the Holy Spirit's direction, things are always in order, even if the order is spontaneous.

Sermons as we know them are unlikely to take place, though teachings are common. In typical Hebrew fashion, these would be dialogues, not monologues. But it is not only the people who have the opportunity to speak out what is in their hearts; the Lord Himself is able to speak *through* each one to others. As God's Spirit leads the meeting, many will share and their short words will form a tapestry of God's message for that time and place. This may include prophetic songs, words of knowledge, or tongues with interpretation. Because people will become *participants* rather than *spectators*, the group members will grow in leadership and gifting. A home meeting is an ideal place for each person to learn how to minister to others, pray for the sick, prophesy over others, and see miracles.

The New Covenant accounts and literature of the first century show a passion in the early believers that has been lost in most of 21st century Christianity. They were passionately convinced of the truth of the Good News. They realized people would go to hell without it. There was no compromise in their message. These first believers presented a gospel that demanded a clear choice! Their passion was not reserved for a weekly meeting. It was 24/7. It affected every area of their lives, everyone they met, everything they did. This was not limited to pastors and evangelists. *All* were equipped to share the Good News and to walk in the miraculous. They were totally surrendered to Messiah.

As this first congregation's passion is restored, miracles will become common in home groups that are yielded to God's Spirit. Believers will be added continually because they will be attracted to the love and unity within the group. People are love-starved and need to experience God's Kingdom demonstrated on earth. Everyone will be a productive, functioning member. Everyone will find their gifts and use them. These house congregations will meet corporately for worship and impartation from those in the city-wide leadership. I envision football stadiums packed with believers celebrating the biblical festivals. I see these gatherings becoming so large they will be featured on the secular television news!

New Wineskins

Many in the Church today feel a godly discontent. We know that the old manna no longer tastes good. We are crying out for something more. We hunger for greater intimacy with God. Our old wineskins cannot contain the glory that is coming to the Church. The master of the feast told the bridegroom at the wedding in Cana, *"You have kept the good wine until now"* (see John 2:10). The best wine, a type of the Holy Spirit, is about to be poured out. But the old system (institutional Christianity or church) will not contain the glory. We need a new wineskin (see Matt. 9:17). God is preparing to release His champion, His One New Man, for the last lap. But first the wineskins must be changed to contain the outpouring of His Spirit.

Lord, You know I don't have all the answers, but You do. You love Your Church. Please restore to us the joy of our salvation. Replace our old wineskins with new wineskins so that when You pour out Your Spirit, we can receive all that You have for us. Give us the courage to scrap the man-made foundations in order to be able to contain the glory of the One New Man anointing. Show us what it means to put on the One New Man (see Ephesians 4:24).

13

TRUTH OR CONSEQUENCES

GOD'S WORD COMMANDS us to pray for the peace of Jerusalem. *"Pray for the peace of Jerusalem: 'May they **prosper** who love you'"* (Ps. 122:6). The word *prosper* refers to something more important than money. In Hebrew it means "heart peace." *Jerusalem* means "City of Peace." One day soon Yeshua will rule Jerusalem, and the Word of the Lord will be broadcast from that city to the whole world. (See Isaiah 2:1-4.)

When we pray for the peace of Jerusalem, we are praying for the return of Messiah Yeshua. We are praying for Jerusalem to become the true City of Peace. We are praying for worldwide revival. We are praying for Jewish unbelievers to be saved so the world can believe. We are praying for the completion of the One New Man.

The devil and his crowd are doing everything possible to abort God's plan. Yeshua said that He would not return until the Jewish people say, *"Blessed is He who comes in the name of the Lord"* (Matt. 23:39). But this does not concern the devil as much as the great harvest that will come when the Jewish branch is grafted back into the olive tree. It will cause the life of God to explode through His One New Man to a dying humanity (see Rom. 11:15).

Dividing the Sheep from the Goats

The plumb line for the church and the nations is always Israel. Genesis 12:3, where God promises to bless those who bless the Jewish people and curse those who curse them, is still true, especially at this set time to favor Zion!

All the earth is the Lord's, and He has assigned Israel to the Jewish people. A summary of His mandate is found in Psalm 105:8–11. God says that He gives the land of Israel (Canaan) to the Jewish people "forever," for "everlasting," and "for a thousand generations." Three different ways He says the same thing. It must be important. A biblical Zionist believes the Jewish people are given the land of Israel forever. Obviously, God was the first Zionist.

God says in Matthew 25:31-46 that nations will be divided as a shepherd separates goats from sheep. A goat has a mind of its own, but a sheep follows the shepherd. Yeshua tells us what the dividing line will be: *"Assuredly, I say to you, inasmuch as you did it to one of the least of these My brethren* [Greek means "from the womb"—the Jewish people], *you did it to Me"* (Matt. 25:40).

The same single judgment issue is mentioned prophetically in Joel 3:2:

> *I will also gather all nations…and **I will enter into judgment** with them there **on account of My people, My heritage Israel, whom they have scattered among the nations,** they have also divided up My land.*

Warning Judgments

The United States, as a nation, has violated every one of the Ten Commandments. We are hanging by a single thread. One of the main reasons we still enjoy some of God's favor is because we are friends with Israel. However, we are dangerously close to losing that blessing. God always warns us before He sends judgment, to allow an opportunity for repentance. He is giving His final warning to America. *"Anyone who harms you* [Israel] *harms my most precious possession. I* [God] *will raise my fist to crush them"* (Zech. 2:8-9 NLT).

John McTernan, in his book *God's Final Warning to America*, documents that when America has turned against Israel we have suffered "warning judgments."[1] McTernan has found hundreds of examples, many coming within 24 hours of the anti-Semitic action. The first President George Bush initiated his 1991 peace plan for the Middle East right after the Gulf War. As part of that plan, he tried to pressure Israel to surrender land for peace. God promised this land to the Jewish people forever. Is it just a coincidence that, despite enjoying historically high approval ratings after the Gulf War, Bush lost his bid for reelection?

When the United States pressures Israel to give away her land, warning judgments befall America almost simultaneously. Proverbs 26:2 says that *"a curse without cause shall not alight."*

- On October 30, 1991, the first President Bush gave a speech to open the "land for peace" conference in Madrid, Spain. The next day, one of the most powerful storms that had ever occurred in the United States smashed into New England. The storm damaged the East Coast from Maine to Florida. Thirty-foot waves pounded President Bush's home in Kennebunkport, Maine, inflicting heavy damage.² A book and a movie were written about this massive storm called *The Perfect Storm*.

- On August 23, 1992, the Madrid Peace Conference was transferred to Washington DC. During the very first day of the conference, Hurricane Andrew hit southern Florida. At that time, Andrew was the worst natural disaster to ever hit the United States![3]

- John McTernan also sees a connection between the September 11, 2001, terrorist attacks on America and America's treatment of Israel. "Major news sources have since reported that just a few days prior to September 11, the Bush administration had formulated a policy of recognizing a Palestinian state with East Jerusalem as its capital. The Secretary of State was going to notify the Saudi Arabian ambassador of this plan on September 13 and was going to announce it at the UN General Assembly on September 23. The attack on September 11 prevented this from happening. At the very time the U.S. was going to force Israel into coexistence with terrorists that were dedicated to the destruction of the Jewish nation, the U.S. came under attack by the same terrorists!"[4]

- McTernan saw another correlation that occurred in 2004. "From August 13 through September 25, the United States suffered a record four direct hits from powerful hurricanes. During this very time, President Bush was pressuring Israel to divide its covenant land. America pressured Israel to evacuate Jews off the land and the hurricanes forced nine million Americans to evacuate."[5]

- The disastrous Hurricane Katrina in August 2005 was also related to America's treatment of Israel, according to McTernan. "The connection between the U.S. government pressuring Israel to destroy 25 [Jewish] settlements on the covenant land and the destruction by Hurricane Katrina is obvious. Southern Louisiana and the Gulf Coast of Mississippi were destroyed just 14 days after Israel began to remove Jews from the land and seven days after the eviction was completed."[6]

These are just a few of the many warnings. If these are just the warnings, imagine what the judgments will be like. God is serious. Time is running short. As a nation, we need to remain true to His Word and remain true to the nation of Israel.

14

THE END OF THE GENTILE AGE?

ARE WE AT THE END of the Gentile Age? We know the first Church was all Jewish. When the Church was opened to Gentiles, they quickly outnumbered the Jews. At that time, the Church shifted from being a Jewish Church with headquarters in Jerusalem to a Gentile Church with headquarters in Rome. We entered the "Times of the Gentiles."

When I read the history of the first Church in the Book of Acts, I am provoked to jealousy. All the believers were ablaze with the fire of the Holy Spirit. The least of the believers could do the same works Jesus did (see Mark 16:17-18). Being a "normal" believer meant healing the sick, casting out demons, raising the dead, hearing from God, and seeing your prayers answered.

When the first Gentiles were added, the Church was still normal. The wall of separation between Jew and Gentile was removed and the Church operated in power as the One New Man. But as we entered the Times of the Gentiles, the culture, leadership style, and power changed. We stopped being normal. Fewer and fewer Jewish people came to faith.

Down through the centuries, the devil has succeeded in once again causing a great enmity between the Jew and Gentile. Today a great wall of separation still remains between the two. Yet Israel is beginning to recognize that her best friends in the world are the Christians. Could it be that when this wall comes down completely we will be normal and walk in the same power as the first Church?

In 1993, Jonathan Bernis, a Messianic Jewish friend, invited me to join him in a new venture. He rented a theater in St. Petersburg, Russia, and advertised a Jewish music concert. We didn't know if anyone would show up. But to our amazement, the theater was packed. I spoke the first night after the concert. Both Jonathan and I witnessed something we had never seen before. Hundreds of *Jewish* people came *running* to the altar to repent of sin and to accept Yeshua as Messiah. Several thousand Jewish people came to Yeshua as a result of those meetings.

Then God spoke to me in a dream. He said, "More Jewish people will come to know Me through your book than anything you have ever done."

I said, "Oh, my testimony book is finally going to take off."

He replied, "No, your book of Jewish testimonies."

Before I could tell Him I didn't have a book of Jewish testimonies, I woke up. I immediately collected ten Jewish testimonies and published a book, *They Thought for Themselves.* History has proven that the dream was from God. We have distributed over half a million of these books, in six different languages, to Jewish people throughout the world. In the former Soviet Union, we mailed the book to a list of Jewish names and addresses the KGB had published on the Internet! Since 1993, hundreds of thousands of Jewish people have come to Yeshua as a result of evangelistic meetings and those books. (See the back of this book for information on how to order *They Thought for Themselves.*) Why is there such openness to the Gospel among Jewish people? We are at the end of the Gentile Age!

Paul prophesied what will happen when Jewish people converge with Christians in Yeshua. *"Now if their* [Jewish people's] *fall is riches for the world, and their failure riches for the Gentiles, how **much more** their full-ness!"* (Rom. 11:12). In other words, Paul says that when the majority of the Jewish people rejected their Messiah, it resulted in the riches of salvation for the Gentiles. But when they receive their Messiah, it will result in *much more* for the Gentiles. This *much more* will be a restoration of the power of the first Church.

Paul further teaches that the majority of the Jewish people will be blinded to the Gospel until the fullness of the Gentiles has come in:

> *For I do not desire brethren, that you should be ignorant of this **mystery**, lest you should be wise in your own opinion, that **blindness in part** has happened to Israel until the **fullness of the Gentiles** has come in. And so all Israel will be saved, as it is written: "The Deliverer will come out of Zion, and He will turn away ungodliness from Jacob"* (Rom. 11:25-26).

This mystery is revealed when we understand the Greek word for *fullness*. The Greek word is *pleroma*, which generally refers to the "totality of God's powers."[1] The same Greek word for fullness is found in Ephesians 4:13: "*...till we all come to the...knowledge of the Son of God...to a **perfect** [mature] man...the **fullness** of [Messiah]....*" In other words, the "fullness of the Gentiles" will come about when the Gentiles reach maturity in their knowledge of Messiah. Part of this maturity will be the restoration of the One New Man as the Gentiles reach out to the Jewish people. At the same time, spiritual blindness will be removed from Jewish eyes. When Jew and Gentile come together as

One New Man, their union will trigger the anointing for the fullness of God and be the catalyst for worldwide revival! God wants you to be so full of Messiah that His anointing will greatly impact the Jewish people who God has cross your path.

The Puritan church fathers found this removal of spiritual scales and the fullness of the Gentiles as no mystery.

In 1652…eighteen of the most eminent Puritan divines…affirmed their belief:

> the Scripture speaks of a *double conversion* of the Gentiles, the first before the conversion of the Jewes, they being the *Branches which are wilde by nature* grafted into the *True Olive Tree* instead of the *naturall Branches* which are broken off. This fulness of the Gentiles shall come in before the conversion of the *Jewes*, and till then blindness hath happened unto Israel, Rom. 11:25. The second, after the conversion of the Jewes…[2]

In other words, they believed that after the Times of the Gentiles, there will be a Jewish revival that will trigger a second Gentile revival. They were speaking of the One New Man!

Thomas Boston, the faithful witness in the unsympathetic General Assembly of the Church of Scotland, said:

Are you longing for a revival to the churches, now lying like dry bones, would you fain have the Spirit of life enter into them? Then pray for the Jews. 'For if the casting away of them be the reconciling of the world; what shall the receiving of them be, but life from the dead.' That will be a lively time, a time of a great outpouring of the Spirit, that will carry reformation to a greater height than yet has been...[3]

Here Boston quotes Romans 11:15, which contains a great blessing for the Gentiles. "What is this 'life from the dead' for Gentiles? It is 'life out of death' (PNT) or Gentile revival!"

Charles Spurgeon, England's best-known and most loved preacher in 1855 said the same thing. "...We do not attach sufficient importance to the restoration of the Jews. We do not think enough of it. But certainly, if there is anything promised in the Bible it is this."[4] He did not place the conversion of the Jews at the consummation of history but rather at the beginning of a period of general revival:

The day shall yet come when the Jews, who were the first apostles to the Gentiles, the first missionaries to us who were afar off, shall be gathered in again. Until that shall be, the fulness of the church's glory can never come. Matchless benefits to the world are bound up with the restoration of Israel; their gathering in shall be as life from the dead.[5]

As I mentioned earlier, Paul explains the timing for this restoration of the Jewish people to the Body of Messiah. He says that the spiritual veil on Jewish people will be lifted at the "fullness" of the Gentiles (see Rom. 11:25). Jesus also refers to the fulfillment of the Times of the Gentiles in Luke 21:24b: *"Jerusalem will be trampled by Gentiles until the **times of the Gentiles are fulfilled**."* In 1967, for the first time since Jesus made that prediction, the Jewish people regained possession of Jerusalem. God is beginning to remove the curse of spiritual blindness over the eyes of the Jewish people.

At the same time, the blindness is also being removed from the eyes of the Gentiles. God's revelation of the mystery concerning the Jewish people and Israel is being downloaded to Gentile Christians. Why now? Gentile Christians are called by God to evangelize the Jew (see Rom. 11:11). And the devil is getting ready for his final attempt to murder the Jewish people in order to prevent the return of Yeshua to Jerusalem. Jeremiah calls it the "time of Jacob's trouble" (see Jer. 30:6-7). It will be the worst persecution of Jewish people in history. We can clearly see the supernatural hatred for the Jew and Israel daily increasing worldwide in the media.

At this set time to favor Zion (see Ps. 102:13-14), few are boldly proclaiming the gospel to Jewish people. Many love the Jewish people, but *love without sharing Yeshua is the worst kind of anti-Semitism!* Some may consider these words harsh, but look at what is happening. I hear excuses like, "Jewish people have suffered enough at the hands of so-called Christians. I don't want to offend them with the gospel. Let's just love them." Many of these "bless Israel" people say, "Of course, I'll share Yeshua with any Jewish person who *asks*." This is a tragedy! In my 30-plus years of Jewish ministry, no Jewish person has *ever* asked me about Jesus! Please take a moment and meditate on the words of Paul, the apostle to the Gentiles:

I have great sorrow and continual grief in my heart. For I could wish that I myself were accursed from [Messiah] *for my brethren, my countrymen according to the flesh....Brethren, my heart's desire and prayer to God for Israel is that they may be saved....How then shall they call on Him in whom they have not believed? And how shall they believe in Him of whom they have **not heard**? And how shall they hear without a preacher? Faith comes from **hearing**...* (Romans 9:2-3; 10:1,14,17).

15

FOR SUCH A TIME AS THIS

BELIEVE the Book of Esther is *the* end-time book for the Church. God is the real hero in this book, although His name is not even mentioned. There are four main characters: Ahasuerus (the Gentile king), Esther (the Jewish queen), Mordecai (who adopted, raised, and nurtured Esther), and Haman (who hated the Jewish people). Esther is symbolic of the Gentile Church, and Mordecai is symbolic of the Messiah. Although Esther became queen, she remained totally obedient to Mordecai.

Jewish people have two names. We have a Hebrew name and a name from our homeland. For instance, my English name is Sid and my Hebrew name is Israel. Esther's Hebrew name was Hadassah, which means "myrtle" (an aromatic shrub), and her Persian name was Ishtar (anglicized to Esther). Ishtar was the name of the pagan fertility goddess. However, Ishtar, when translated into Hebrew means, "to hide."

Esther was a beautiful virgin, an orphan who had such supernatural favor that she rose to royalty. In Yeshua, the Gentile Church is a beautiful virgin. Though adopted (grafted in), Gentiles have risen to become kings and queens in God's Kingdom. The Church, like Esther, has hidden her Jewish roots and is dressed in Persian, Ishtar clothes. Originally, Esther wore Jewish dress. But when she became a Persian queen, it was necessary for Esther to put on Gentile clothes. In a similar way, it was necessary for God to move the early Church out of its original Jewish dress to reach Gentiles. But Esther, we are at the end of the Gentile Age. Is it not time to change your clothes and your name? Is it not time to stop hiding?

Esther is a book of split-second timing and instant obedience. This is why her preparation was so necessary for this *kairos* moment. Before going to the king, Esther had to soak in oil of myrrh for six months. The myrrh shrub is bitter on the outside, but sweet on the inside. The soaking allowed her spirit (inside) to dominate her flesh (outside). Then she soaked in perfumes for another six months. Esther, Church, as you spend time soaking in God's presence, you will change. This preparation for your appointment with the King will make the difference between being in the outer court and becoming His Bride.

After Esther soaked for a year, she thought she was ready, but God knew better. She had to wait another three years before she went to the king. She had an opportunity to get bitter or better. After all, she was beautiful and gifted, yet seemingly placed on a shelf. Spiritually speaking, she could have been like the five foolish virgins of Matthew 25. Instead, like the five wise virgins, she prepared herself to meet the king by cultivating humility and intimacy with God.

The Haman Spirit

Haman, the prime minister of Persia and second in command, erected a gallows to hang Mordecai after Mordecai refused to bow down to him. However, just as the tree raised to crucify Yeshua resulted in the deathblow to the devil, the tree raised to hang Mordecai resulted in Haman's death (see 1 Cor. 2:8).

Haman's ancestors were the Amalekites. God knew the Amalekites would be used to fight the Jewish people throughout history. This is why He said in Exodus 17:16, *"The Lord will have war with Amalek from generation to generation."* The Haman spirit is rising up again worldwide. The Amalekite (Haman) spirit even rests under the surface in America. Watch as the Jewish people are blamed for the next economic collapse in America. Haman bribed the king with ten thousand talents of silver for permission to destroy all the Jews. This Amalekite spirit controls the United Nations as well as the U.S. State Department. What will you do, Esther, when the oil-rich Arab countries say we must reject Israel or we will have no gasoline?

The Hadassah Anointing

In the Book of Esther, we see that the devil's strategy was to murder *all* the Jewish people. Throughout the Bible and the history of mankind, satan has always attempted to annihilate Jews from the earth. Satan believed that if he could destroy the Jews, he could prevent the coming of the Messiah. Even after Yeshua came, satan has tried to destroy the Jews because he understands the significance of the One New Man. Without the Jews, there will be no One New Man.

Queen Esther was the *only* one who could go to the king to save the Jewish people. She could have just enjoyed her life of royalty without taking any risks. Some in the Church today continue to soak in the anointing and do nothing. Esther knew that it was life-threatening to reveal her Jewish connection. But it would have been more dangerous to keep quiet. Mordecai warned Esther: *"Do not think in your heart that you will escape in the king's palace any more than all the other Jews"* (Esther 4:13). Some Gentiles might think anti-Semitism doesn't affect them. But after the devil attacks the Jews, he will come after the Christians.

> *For if you remain completely silent at this time, relief and deliverance will arise for the Jews from another place, but you and your father's house will perish. Yet who knows whether you have come to the kingdom for such a time as this?* (Esther 4:14).

The Book of Esther takes place in Persia, now known as Iran. The same Haman spirit is active in Iran today as well as in Russia. Ezekiel 38 describes the alignment of Iran, Russia, and other nations against Israel. Considering the threat of modern nuclear weapons, Israel does not stand a chance (apart from God).

Although in the natural the destruction of the Jewish people in the Book of Esther was sealed, Esther tapped into the higher laws of the invisible kingdom. After prayer and fasting, a great miracle took place. Instead of being annihilated, the Jewish people *"overpowered those who hated them"* (Esther 9:1). Since the Jewish people were armed with the "sword," a type of the Word of God (see Esther 9:5), revival broke out among the Gentiles (see Esther 8:17).

Today, things are as serious and life threatening for the Jewish people as in the days of the Book of Esther. I pray in Yeshua's name that you receive the same anointing that was on Queen Esther—the Hadassah anointing! I pray that you stand up and intercede as Esther did for the life of the Jewish people. *"Yet who knows whether you have come to the kingdom for such a time as this?"* (Esther 4:14).

God's pattern is the same today. Salvation has come to the Gentile Church:

- To provoke the Jew to jealousy.

- To form the One New Man.

- To restore the Church to her original power.

- *To save the world.*

ENDNOTES

Chapter 1: The Jewish Covenant
1. *Merriam-Webster Online*, s.v. "convergence," http://www. m-w.com/cgi-bin/dictionary (accessed August 8, 2006).

Chapter 2: "We Are Not Lost"
1. Robert D. Heidler, "The Messianic Church: Discovering Our Lost Inheritance," unpublished manuscript © 2000, p. 12. Heidler refers to the following source: Steven Silbiger, *The Jewish Phenomenon: Seven Keys to the Enduring Wealth of a People*, Atlanta: Longstreet Press, 2000, p. 2.
2. Silberger, p. 4, as cited in Heidler, p. 12.

Chapter 3: The Rabbinic Conspiracy
1. Kevin Howard and Marvin Rosenthal, *The Feasts of the Lord* (Nashville: Thomas Nelson Publishers, 1997), 126.
2. Dan Gruber, *Rabbi Akiba's Messiah* (Hanover, NH: Elijah Publishing, 1999), 80. Gruber's book provides an excellent history of the origins of Rabbinic Judaism.
3. Ibid.
4. Quoted in J. M. Baumgarten, "The Unwritten Law in the Pre-Rabbinic Period," *Journal for the Study of Judaism in the Persian, Hellenistic and Roman Period*, 3 (October 1972): 23, quoted in Gruber, 107.
5. Gruber, 111, 116-118.
6. Raymond Robert Fischer, *Full Circle* (Tiberias, Israel: Olim Publications, 2002), 56.
7. Ron Cantor, *I Am Not Ashamed* (Gaithersburg, MD: Tikkun International, 1999), 140-141.
8. Ibid., 142.
9. For the commentaries of the rabbis before Yeshua and the revisionary views of the modern rabbis on the major Messianic prophecies, read Philip Moore, *The End of History,*

Messiah Conspiracy (Atlanta: Ramshead Press International, 1996).

Chapter 4: Who Is Israel?

1. Derek Prince, *Prophetic Destinies* (Altamonte Springs, FL: Creation House, 1992), 13.

2. Derek Prince, Foreword to *Time Is Running Short* by Sid Roth (Shippensburg, PA: Destiny Image Publishers, 1990).

3. Over the years some have objected to my use of the term "Gentile Christian." I meet many Christians who are ashamed of their Gentile heritage and wish they were Jewish. Some feel that the term *Gentile* is even derogatory. While the word *Gentiles* has sometimes been associated with "heathen," it is better defined as "nations" or "non-Jews"—a distinct people group. The term is neutral. There are good Gentiles and bad Gentiles, just as there are good Jews and bad Jews. Besides, Paul would not have addressed non-Jewish believers as "Gentiles" if it were an insult. (See Romans 11:13; 16:4; Galatians 2:12,14.)

   Should we let unbelievers define our identity? Although I am a new creation in Yeshua, I am not ashamed of my Jewish heritage. If I were a Gentile, I would not be ashamed of my Gentile heritage. But I would be proud of my identity. Our *heritage* is Jewish or Gentile, but our *identity* is Yeshua!

Chapter 6: Christian?

1. One example of a church leader who stood up for the Jewish people was Dietrich Bonhoeffer, a German Lutheran minister whose refusal to recant his opposition to Adolph Hitler's Nazi regime led to his imprisonment and eventual execution. He openly opposed not only the Nazi's anti-Jewish policies but also the Church's acquiescence to those policies.

2. Unless otherwise noted, the following historical references are from Steffi Rubin, *Anti-Semitism* (n.p.: Hineni Ministries, 1977), 32-33.

3. John Chrysostom, quoted in X. Malcolm Hay, *Europe and the Jews* (Boston: Beacon Press, 1961), 27.

4. F.E. Talmage, ed., *Disputation and Dialogue: Readings in the Jewish-Christian Encounter* (New York: Ktav Publishing House, Inc., 1975), 18.

5. Martin Luther, quoted in *Encyclopaedia Judaica*, vol. 8 (Jerusalem: Keter Publishing House Jerusalem Ltd., 1972), 692.

Luther instructed "rulers who have Jewish subjects [to] exercise a sharp mercy toward these wretched people....They must act like a good physician who, when gangrene has set in, proceeds without mercy to cut, saw, and burn flesh, veins, bone, and marrow....Burn down their synagogues.... If this does not help we must drive them out like mad dogs." From *Luther's Works, Vol. 47: The Christian in Society IV* (Philadelphia: Fortress Press, 1971), 268-293. Excerpts quoted in the *Internet Medieval Sourcebook* www.fordham. edu/halshall/source/luther-jews.html (accessed March 28, 2007).

6. *Encyclopaedia Judaica*, vol. 8, 693.

7. Adolph Hitler, *Mein Kampf*, translated by Ralph Manheim (Boston: Houghton Mifflin Co., 1971), 65.

8. True repentance is not just saying you are sorry. It involves a change of behavior.

Chapter 7: The Constantine Conspiracy

1. Raymond Robert Fischer, *The Children of God: Messianic Jews and Gentile Christians Nourished by Common Jewish Roots* (Tiberias, Israel: Olim Publications, 2000), 47.

2. Constantine, quoted in Theodoret, *Historia Ecclesiastica 1*, 10.

3. Quoted in Lars Enarson, "The Feast of Passover and Intercession for Salvation of the Jewish People: An Appeal for an All Night Prayer Vigil on April 7 or 8, 2001" (The Watchman International, P.O. Box 3670, Pensacola, FL 32516, 1999), 1-2.

4. "In the fifth century the western church [Roman Catholic] ordered it to be celebrated forever on the day of the old Roman feast of the birth of Sol [sun]" *The Encyclopedia Americana*, 1942 Edition, vol. 6, 623.

5. *Century Dictionary and Cyclopedia*, 1903, vol. 2, 987.

6. Tertullian, *Against Marcion 1*, ANF III, 271.

7. Justin Martyr, *Dialogue 21*,1; 23,3.

8. See Fischer's book *The Children of God* for a more detailed history of the first church.

Chapter 8: Biblical Festivals—Blessing or Bondage?

1. A traditional understanding of the Passover *seder* ties the four cups of wine to the four "I will" statements of Exodus 6:6–7: *"Therefore say to the children of Israel: 'I am the Lord; I will bring you out from under the burdens of the Egyptians, I will rescue you from their bondage, and I will redeem you with an outstretched arm and with great judgments. I will take you as My people, and I will be your God....'"* "*I will redeem you*" is the third statement, which corresponds to the third cup.

Chapter 9: Celebrate the Feasts

1. Dr. John Fischer, *The Meaning and Importance of the Jewish Holidays*, copyright © 1979. For more information, contact Menorah Ministries, P.O. Box 669, Palm Harbor, FL 34682.

2. There is ample indication that Yeshua Himself probably instituted this practice, which then found its way into traditional observance because of the early Messianic Jews.

3. C.F. Lampe, *A Patristic Greek Lexicon*.

4. See Hayyim Schauss, *The Jewish Festivals: A Guide to Their History and Observance* (New York: Schocken Books, 1996), 95.

5. For more information, read Joseph Hertz's book *Daily Prayer Book* 865.

6. Both are references to Messiah, seed and branch of David (cf. Isa. 9:5-6; Jer. 23:5-6).

7. See previous endnote.

Chapter 10: The Law of Evangelism

1. John Owen quoted in I.D.E. Thomas, *A Puritan Golden Treasury of Quotations* (Carlisle, PA: Banner of Truth Trust,

1977) 155, 157, quoted in Michael Brown, *Our Hands Are Stained with Blood* (Shippensburg, PA: Destiny Image, 1992), 20.

Chapter 13: Truth or Consequences

1. John McTernan, *God's Final Warning to America* (Oklahoma City, OK: Hearthstone Publishing, 2000), 82–119.

2. Timothy Snodgrass, "History and Future of USS New Madrid," http://www.etpv.org/2002/histand.html (accessed May 19, 2004).

3. Ibid.

4. John McTernan, "Israel Connection," Messianic Vision Newsletter, No. 0301, January 2003.

5. John McTernan, *As America Has Done to Israel*, (Longwood, FL: Xulon Press, 2006), 203.

6. John McTernan, "The Katrina-Israel Connection," Messianic Vision Newsletter, No. 0506, November 2005.

Chapter 14: The End of the Gentile Age?

1. *Wikipedia*, s.v. "pleroma," http://en.wikipedia.org/wiki/Pleroma (accessed March 28, 2007).

2. Ian H. Murray, *The Puritan Hope; Revival and the Interpretation of Prophecy*, (Edinburgh, UK: Banner of Truth Trust, 1971), 72 (available at 3 MKurrayfield Rd, Edinburgh, UK, or P.O. Box 621, Carlisle, PA), quoted in Dan Gruber, *The Church and the Jews: The Biblical Relationship* (Hanover, NH: Elijah Publishing, 1997), 310-311.

3. Tomas Boston, quoted in Murray, 113, quoted in Gruber, 312.

4. Charles Spurgeon , quoted in Murray, 214,quoted in Gruber, 316.

5. Ibid., 256 , quoted in Gruber, 316. "Vol. 17, p. 703-704."

Write for our free newsletter and catalog:
Messianic Vision
P.O. Box 1918
Brunswick, GA 31521-1918
Telephone: 912-265-2500
Fax: 912-265-3735
E-mail: info@sidroth.org

Visit Sid's web site: www.SidRoth.org for the following great resources...
Check Sid's speaking itinerary
Watch online or download episodes of his television program, *It's Supernatural!*
Listen online or download archives of his radio show, *Messianic Vision*—or subscribe to the podcast!
Shop an online catalog jam-packed with mentoring tools and resource materials.
Enjoy a library of articles on topics such as Jewish roots, the One New Man, Israel updates, powerful prayer, supernatural healing and experiencing the presence of God
and much, much more!

THEY THOUGHT FOR THEMSELVES

The people in this book come from widely divergent backgrounds including a holocaust survivor, a multimillionaire, a media executive and a Ph.D. They range in upbringing from atheist to Orthodox.

What is the common denominator among those in this unusual group?

They all thought for themselves and they dared to confront the forbidden.

ISBN 0-910267-02-2

Cost: A donation of $15.00, which includes shipping.

You can order the book by calling 1-800-548-1918 or by visiting www.SidRoth.org.

Additional copies of this book and other
book titles from Destiny Image are
available at your local bookstore.

Call toll-free: 1-800-722-6774.

Send a request for a catalog to:

Destiny Image® Publishers, Inc.
P.O. Box 310
Shippensburg, PA 17257-0310

*"Speaking to the Purposes of God for This
Generation and for the Generations to Come"*

**For a complete list of our titles,
visit us at www.destinyimage.com**

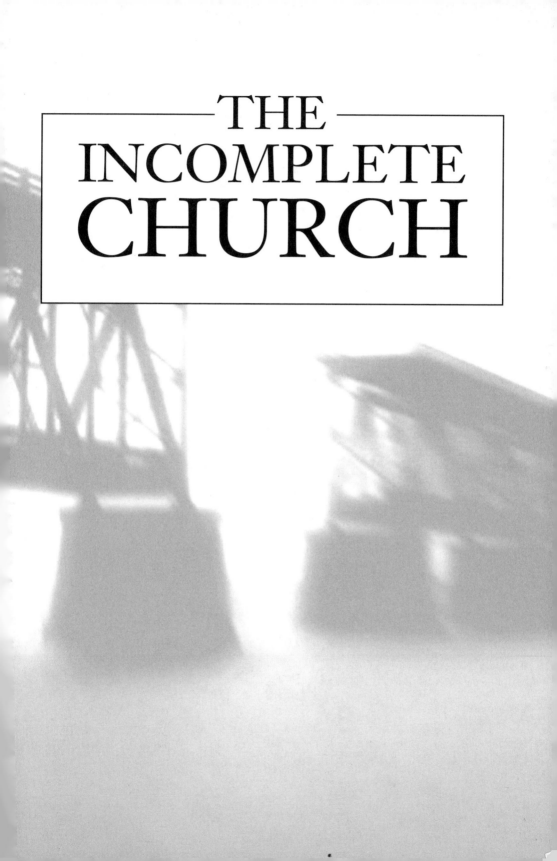

THE
INCOMPLETE
CHURCH